MW01089083

What Readers Say

This book is a must-read for anyone who wants to ensure the wealth they leave their family has a positive impact. It offers valuable tools for families including how to get along, appreciate each other for each member's talents and for developing the trust needed to be in harmony.

—Pete Coors
Chairman, Coors Brewing Company

As a wealth management professional, I recognize that merely focusing on creating or preserving financial wealth for the families we work with is short-changing our clients. Families of wealth also yearn for wise counsel on how their financial wealth can be a force for good - for future generations and for the communities where they live. Bridging Generations *is an indispensable guidebook for those families.*

—Neil Douthat, CPWA
Senior Vice President, Wealth Management
UBS Financial Services, Inc.

I would unequivocally recommend this book as mandatory reading for any G1 or G2 families of wealth who are concerned about having a successful transition of the family legacy between generations.

As is often pointed out in this communiqué the majority of transitions are unsuccessful as a result of a lack of preparedness by the heirs: understanding the dynamics of being the curators of wealth for successive generations.

This book highlights the steps the family needs to take to reduce the odds of the shirtsleeves-to-shirtsleeves phenomenon.

My family and I worked with TWG for several years learning and practicing the steps outlined here. With this work, I am confident we have established a way forward that preserves all of the family assets, including the most important: care, love and unity.

Congratulations to Roy and Amy for this important piece of work.

—Peter E. Gilgan
Founder and CEO, Mattamy Homes, Ltd.

Roy William's latest, Bridging Generations *is a great primer for families who want to transition a business to the next generation and keep the family values intact. Our family got not only the pathways outlined in the book, we also got the wis-*

dom and guidance of Roy and his professional team to coach and guide us through the early years of putting our transition plan in place.

—**Peter Ganahl**
CEO, Ganahl Lumber Company

We are a family of 18 consisting of G-1, G-2 and G-3's. We have been a client of The Williams Group for several years and have participated in the exercises described in this book. Through working with The Williams Group, our family has grown closer together, developed a mutual respect and greater love for each other. They helped us to more fully know what it means to be a family unit in harmony and to define the purpose of our wealth and the legacy we will leave for our current and future generations. Our children and grandchildren are now much better prepared to successfully lead productive lives while enjoying and preserving the family financial wealth.

—**Charles C. Stephenson, Jr.**
Stephenson Investments, Inc.

In this book, The Williams Group provides information for readers to apply in planning the transfer of their assets to others. The Williams Group has gathered this information from many actual family cases and years of experience. This book is a must for people who wish to learn ways to communicate and transfer their personal mission in life to the recipients of their assets.

—**Glen A. Holden**
US Ambassador (R)

Williams and Castoro address one of the biggest pain points business families face: 70 percent of them will fail at passing their legacies on to the next generation. Since what we leave after we're gone helps give meaning to our lives, every business family needs to know how to be in the thirty percent that makes a successful transition. Drawing on the experiences of more than 3000 business families, the authors know how to do it. They explain what needs to be done, and they do it in practical terms along with riveting examples. This book fills a need! Frankly, I think all business families owe Williams and Castoro a debt of thanks for this book.

—**Mitzi Purdue**
National Speaker, Author
Perdue and Sheraton Hotels Families

Great wealth can be used in a multitude of beneficial ways. The one thing that no amount of wealth can do, however, is insulate us from the "human condition." If not addressed, the human conditions of emotionality, aspiration, conflict and mortality can poison all of the potential that wealth presents. In my work as a wealth management advisor, I have witnessed the heartbreaking destruction of families, individuals – and financial wealth – due to the absence of attention to our natural human tendencies.

Bridging Generations *illuminates this all-too-often overlooked facet of family wealth and refocuses a family's attention and efforts on preserving their true wealth – the individual family members, those living and those not yet born.*

—Frances W. Douthat
Vice President, Wealth Management
Senior Wealth Strategy Associate

Roy Williams and The Williams Group coached our family into the next generation. Peggy and I became coaches, sponsors and teachers for our children while letting them grow into leaders. We learned to give our children a lot of responsibility augmented by trust, respect and love.

We were taught by Roy Williams, Joel Kimmel and Emily Bouchard. We are all eternally grateful.

This book provides the information necessary to navigate the journey and the journey always requires guidance.

—Carl & Peggy Sewell
Founders and Owners, Sewell Automotive

This book outlines the expectations for the members of a family starting with the meetings. The Williams Group Process created an atmosphere for our multi-generational family to have honest communications and lasting tools for the following years.

—Anne Wiles
Franchisee of Carl's Jr., fast food restaurant company

This book is full of useful examples, understandable explanations and detailed checklists. Its emphasis on the need to balance family trust and inclusiveness with accountability and mentoring separates this wealth transfer book from others on that subject.

—James C. Pigott
Industrialist and Philanthropist

Communicating between generations can be very difficult. Communicating between family members with different histories and financial needs can be impossible, especially after the patriarch dies. The Williams Group gave us the secret sauce and a process for resolving our family issues. I wish we had gone to them earlier and I am grateful we went to them when we did.

—Bill Meek
Chairman of the Board, Meek's Lumber and Hardware

This book is a gift to all who are interested in protecting not just family wealth but also family harmony. The Williams Group has designed a clear and defined path for families to build trust and communication as well as to plan for the future. I know so many families who did not go through a planning process until a triggering event occurred such as the death of a father. Unfortunately, what follows is often a disruptive and chaotic time for all family members. Our family was lucky enough to find Roy Williams and embark proactively on the Preparing Heirs process. While not always easy, we now feel united, resilient and, most of all, prepared.

—Carrie Meek-Cuneo
President, Western Division
Meek's Lumber and Hardware

Transitions are never easy. Generation bridging is amongst the hardest to successfully accomplish where wealth, personalities and generational values collide. Roy Williams and Amy Castoro offer sound guidance to mitigate the inevitable family distress surrounding generational transitions.

—Art Ludwick
Owner, Rainbird Manufacturing Company

For most of my 40 years as the family consigliere to America's more affluent families and business owners, my law firm's mission is to protect our clients' assets from financially ruinous lawsuits and to pass the maximum amount of wealth from Generation 1 to Generation 2 and Generation 3 with the least amount of transfer taxation. When I read the earlier book, Preparing Heirs, I realized our work was incomplete unless we engaged the next generations early in the process.

The Williams Group platform in Bridging Generations *presents the best opportunity to avoid the devastating "shirtsleeves-to-shirtsleeves in three generations." While the work is challenging, the results are worth the effort to successfully protect and pass on the family legacy. The Williams Group is the best thing to happen to the estate and trust planning industry since the advent of the asset protection trust.* Bridging Generations *is a must-have guidebook and should be on every serious estate planning professional's desk next to the Internal Revenue Code.*

—Jeff Verdon, Esq.
Verdon Law Group, LLP

Every family business will face difficult and emotionally charged challenges beyond expected corporate concerns. I doubt they will prevail without the honest conversations and heart based trust and communication skills that Roy and The Williams Group coaches teach their family clients.

—Caroline Daniels
Retired Chairman and CEO
Aircraft Technical Publishers

Roy and Amy's book, Bridging Generations, *helps families comprehend and appreciate what ultimately matters – the principles, ethics and morals that define reputation and cement legacy. This book serves as an invaluable tool in educating families about the importance of having a concerted familial mission;* Bridging Generations *expresses, in a thoughtful and legible manner, this vital cohesion and healthy effects that can result in positively linking generations.*

—Thorne L. Perkin
President, Papamarkou Asset Management, Inc., New York

My experience with Roy Williams *and his group has been invaluable helping me organize my thoughts for what a real family future wealth plan is. I was very confused on what I was trying to accomplish until I had the chance to understand what the real goals and objectives are for me and my family.*

Bridging Generations *is a great insight into the realities of forming and shaping our families' history.* Preparing Heirs *is a great book and helped me tremendously.* Bridging Generations *is a terrific push forward.*

—Richard (Dick) Patterson
The Patterson Family

Roy and Amy have presented many facets of trust, communications, values, and beliefs like a diamond being carefully cut to expose its brilliance of light glittering before your eyes, thus capturing the essence of a worthy cause of planning and transitioning for a family's wealth and sustainable legacy.

Bridging Generations… *drives home the importance of the entire family's participation emphasizing trust, effective communications, and accountability to achieve transitioning family wealth and values for a sustainable legacy.*

Being a past recipient of The Williams Group's teachings, Bridging Generations… *is a wonderful refresher of lessons learned and a great reference as the plan for a sustainable transition of wealth and values plays out over time.*

Bridging Generations… *is a comprehensive manuscript designed to develop family trust, effective communications, values, and beliefs to enhance the planning process for a successful transitioning of wealth, values and a sustainable family legacy.*

—Richard D. Boyd
Co-CEO and President, Boyd Coffee Company

This book provides some very useful research data and insights, not only for families of wealth, but advisors working with these families.

The Williams Group research identifies as the main cause of failure in transitioning family wealth the breakdown in communication and trust within the family unit. Their research, as well as other published findings, reveals that these wealth transitions have only a thirty percent success rate.

Of particular interest to me is the role of family philanthropy. I am not sur-

prised that it is a common element among families with successful transitions. The values and skills needed for effective and meaningful philanthropy – good communication, trust, accountability, consensus building, as well as articulated shared values – are also necessary for success in transitioning family wealth.

—Marvi Ricker
VP, Philanthropic Advisory Services
BMO Wealth Management

Many of those considering the services of The Williams Group are planning for the transition of wealth that was built through business and enterprise. While building that wealth in business these founders and leaders never presupposed the success of their endeavors without fully sharing with their employees, their teams, the vision prior to executing any plan. These leaders built wealth by working within teams to strategize and plan so that team members knew their roles then executed the plan. So too with the transition of wealth. The vision of many parents is that as they pass on, what they have built be used to create opportunity for their children that is greater than what they themselves had. That their children use it to grow themselves and do greater work. Not just grow the wealth or preserve it, but use it to grow the person and purpose. Now actively transitioning wealth, how can one expect the next generation to fulfill that vision of person and purpose if they haven't participated in the plan created by one who is no longer living?

This book and the work of The Williams Group provides a playbook for the successful transition of wealth through the learning and understanding of individuals. They do not leave you to decipher the playbook alone, they provide the coaching to successfully execute the transition and preservation of wealth to the furtherance of the family in future generations.

—Jordan Vander Kolk
President, Artisan Medical Displays

Once again Roy Williams has given us a well-marked path through the minefields of successful wealth transfers. Generational differences are the new hurdles requiring new communication skills. Masterfully, Roy and Amy have laid out a step by step program that will bring the generations together. No one does this better than The Williams Group. Love and understanding are two very different words when we arrive at the chasm of generational differences. Communication is the bridge of understanding. This book shows us step by step how to achieve the harmony that will lead to successful wealth transfers.

—Joe Harper
President and CEO, The Del Mar Thoroughbred Club
Trustee, Cecil B. De Mille Foundation

Roy and Amy simply "get it right." Family founders are amazing at building wealth but rarely trained on how to preserve and pass on their legacy and values. Much of the information surrounding the family office space simply deals with wealth preservation and to some extent, governance structures. That information does not touch on the human aspect of family wealth and transition. Bridging Generations *provides the solid case studies and roadmap for avoiding the pitfalls that so many families end up in. I view this work as a necessary part of the family office toolkit for generational transition.*

—Wendy Craft
COO, Favara Family Office

The last thing all wealth creators want is for their hard work and success to become the instrument of destroying their family. Nor do they want to see the fruits of their labors squandered because of inadequate planning and education. Most would love to see their heirs use what they are given to build even greater success in addition to living full happy lives. Families are complicated organisms and often present a big challenge to decision makers attempting to make equitable, intelligent choices about wealth and responsibility transfer to succeeding generations. Roy Williams and Amy Castoro offer a proven practical process to families needing to navigate this difficult issue.

The best gift that heirs can receive is a family plan that gives them direction about how to co-develop their family values with their family, and properly utilize what they inherit. It is the wealth creator's responsibility to assure this plan is developed as a family team while they are able to participate in developing the process.

—Eddie Bradley
Founder and CEO, AutoInc

Too many wealthy families become embroiled in family trust litigation, particularly after the matriarch's and/or patriarch's passing. This book's process for creating trust and consensus across generations could and should decrease that growing trend.

—Carol Zeist
Family Trust Litigation Attorney, Newmeyer & Dillion, LLP

Louis Pasteur said, "Fortune favors the prepared mind." If you are like many fortunate families today wanting to avoid the statistics of family wealth disappearing within three generations, you will reap the benefit of the accumulated wisdom of Roy Williams and Amy Castoro. There is no better resource for preparing the hearts and minds of whole families for a successful inheritance.

This is wonderful material - especially in a time when wealth creators are inundated with bad counsel by professionals and institutions with vested interests intended to undermine their families.

—**Fred Smith**
President, The Gathering

Families are one of our greatest gifts, but families are vulnerable. For our family, a founding father of a successful company, with four children from two mothers who share equal company ownership, two working in the company, offer unique challenges.

Our first sessions with The William's Group revealed that a lifetime of building a growing business did not provide the unique and personal skills required in transitioning wealth to an unprepared family.

Under The William's Group's professional guidance we discovered a deeper understanding of ourselves and each other, revealing our potential trials, and ultimately strengthening our unity, respect, trust, and family bond. We now have a Mission Statement and a playbook of performance. While The William's Group cannot change individual personalities, they can develop rules for communication and standards identifying acceptable behavior.

Our blood family, our business family, and the communities in which we work will all benefit from a successful transition of our assets. The William's Group has given all of us an opportunity to increase our odds of future success.

Thank you,
The Keiswetter Family

—**Paul Keiswetter**
President and CEO, Petoskey Plastics

Effective communication remains vital (to avoid, e.g., unpleasant surprises), as does preparation for potential fiduciary roles or simply for beneficiaries' prudent management of inherited funds and informed decision making about their own needs, opportunities and goals. Even issues inherent in preserving a testator's vacation home for interested descendants are analogous to those of continuing a family business. Bridging Generations is thus worth recommending to a broad spectrum of persons concerned with estate planning.

—**Edward C. Halbach**
Prof. Emeritus, UC Berkeley School of Law and Janet B. Halbach

This book is an excellent resource for families who are interested in successfully transitioning their wealth to the next generation. Roy Williams and Amy Castoro offer a time-tested approach to a successful transition rooted in building trust and improving communication. As a financial advisor who works with many first-gen-

eration wealth creators, I found this book to be an excellent tool to discuss the "softer" – and just as important - side of wealth transfer.

—Wendy J. Dominguez
President and Cofounder, Innovest Portfolio Solutions, LLC

Bridging Generations *is an incredible testimony to the expertise and lifelong learnings of Roy Williams and his team. It is a must read for family office executives who represent or wish to represent multiple generations. Roy has been a great mentor to me during my family office career. He coached me to be the family consigliere to provide families the much-needed level of support required for a sustainable legacy. That has served me well in working with various families that I have represented over the years.* Bridging Generations *is a great tool and guide designed to assist families and family office executives navigate a road to success built on trust, communication and a clear vision that aligns with the families' values and purpose for their wealth.*

—Chris Cincera
COO and CFO, Family Office

The successful transition of wealth within a family has many challenges as outlined by The Williams Group. These challenges only increase when a family business is also involved. Very often, owners of these businesses want to see the continued success of the business they worked so hard for, ensure that their family wealth is protected, see their children succeed in business and most importantly, they wish to keep the family relationships intact and harmonious.

The book Bridging Generations *by Roy Williams and Amy Castoro of The Williams Group is a vital tool for all families who want to prepare their children to preserve the legacy of business and wealth that is being transferred to them, lead productive and successful lives and keep family relationships intact. The book outlines the importance of family trust, developing good and effective communication and achieving accountability for a continued family legacy. This is a must read for any family hierarchy wishing to begin the process of transitioning a successful business and/or family wealth to the next generation*

—David G. Roberts, MBA
Lead and Principal, The Rainier Group

I highly recommend Bridging Generations - *Transitioning Family Wealth and Values for a Sustainable Legacy to anyone attempting to navigate through the complex world of financial planning for their heirs. As a father to two adult children, the importance of securing my wealth for my family and future generations has in the past few years become paramount. Roy's book provided a road map that*

I could easily follow to ensure that my hard-earned money would remain a part of my legacy.

—Jose Higueras
Tennis Pro and Coach, US Tennis Association

As with Roy's seminal book, Preparing Heirs, *his new book,* Bridging Generations, *co-authored with Amy, helps every enterprising family make a great transition thereby avoiding the "three generation shirtsleeves" proverb for many generations into the future.*

—James (Jay) E. Hughes, Jr., Esq.
Author

Bridging Generations *is a well-written, reader-friendly book. It describes the finely-honed process developed by Roy Williams and his team for building family unity through trust and communication. The idea of a loving, respectful, cohesive multi-generational family may seem like a dream to most, but here is a practical, step-by-step guide to making it a reality.*

—Bob Graham
CEO and Founder, NamasteDirect SF

I have been using the 'team' approach and I realize that people are much more willing to work if they have a part in the game. All the things suggested in this book create harmony within a family.

—Dine Dellenback
Wyoming State Vice Regent Elect for DAR

Roy Williams has dedicated his life to helping families prepare for their wealth transition. It's his higher calling. Through it all, Roy has discovered that authentic trust is the root of all progress for families. It sets them on a higher trajectory. In this definitive book, Roy and Amy share their collective wisdom, knowledge and experience about building trust in families. Having seen their work firsthand, I know what they write of in these pages truly works. So, read this book not only for the knowledge you will gain, but the impact you will deliver and the results you will achieve.

—Bob Gould
Partner, Creaghan McConnell Group

We can reduce the estate tax on a giant estate to zero but there is nothing I can do in my documents to fix broken people.
Working with people is always a challenge but with family in a business it is mission critical.
I have seen firsthand the wonderful work done by The Williams Group in build-

ing harmony into the family and the values.

The alternative is not very pretty. All of us could benefit from Preparing Heirs, Family Meetings, *and now* Bridging Generations!

I wish I had known of The Williams Group 40 years ago!

—**David Allen Brown**
Founding Partner, Brown & Streza, LLP

Bridging Generations *is a must-read book for families of wealth.*

Many families we work with find the most important aspect of wealth management is preparing their children and grandchildren to become high functioning financial adults. Common questions are: How much to give them and when? What is the meaning of money? What purpose does it serve? Will wealth have a negative or positive impact on future generations? The issues become more and more complex with each generation. Some family members are enabled to become dependent; others find their path to self-actualization. How does a family work together to achieve harmony and individual self-actualization using wealth as strength and not a crutch?

Northern Trust and The Williams Group have a track record of successfully helping families reach an understanding of the purpose of their wealth, individually and collectively. How does a family begin this process? My recommendation is to start by reading Bridging Generations. *Then become fiercely intentional by engaging with your family using best practices and expert facilitators.*

Have faith that answers will unfold through your "intentional journey of discovery" as you and your family come together to define your family's values, vision, goals and roles.

—**Betty Mower Potalivo**
Region President, Northern Trust

Wow! – Roy and Amy have written the go-to primer on family business and succession that will keep you engaged, motivated and moved to action for your own family – seeking not only focus on assets but most importantly, the value of family unity and harmony.

—**Dean Daily**
CEO, Van Nuys Airport Industrial Center

There is a very short list of wealth advisors who have the character, wisdom and stature to sincerely and effectively advise families of significant wealth. Roy and his talented team are leaders on this short list. They know how to teach families the essential competencies required to sustain and, when necessary, restore relationships while greatly improving probabilities that wealth, influ-

ence, values and commitments to making a difference will be transitioned to successive generations.

—Michael D. Allen
Board Certified Estate Planning Specialist
Allen-Lottmann-Kimmel PC

BRIDGING
GENERATIONS

Transitioning Family Wealth *and*
Values *for a* Sustainable Legacy

ROY O. WILLIAMS
and
AMY A. CASTORO

HIGHERLIFE
PUBLISHING & MARKETING
www.ahigherlife.com

Bridging Generations—Transitioning Family Wealth and Values for a
  Sustainable Legacy
By: Roy O. Williams and Amy A. Castoro

Published by HigherLife Development Services, Inc.
PO Box 623307
Oviedo, Florida 32762
(407) 563-4806
www.ahigherlife.com

Copyright © 2017 Roy O. Williams and Amy A. Castoro
All rights reserved
ISBN 13: 978-0-9989773-1-7
ISBN-10: 0-9989773-1-4

No part of this book may be reproduced without written permission from the publisher or copyright holder, who holds the copyright except for a reviewer who may quote brief passages in a review; nor may any part of this book be transmitted in any form or by any means electronic, mechanical, photocopying, recording, or other, without prior written permission from the publisher or copyright holder.

This book is sold with the understanding that the subject matter covered herein does not constitute legal, accounting, or other professional advice for any specific individual or situation. Anyone planning to take action in any of the areas this book describes should seek professional advice from accountants, lawyers, tax advisors, and other advisors, as would be prudent and advisable under their given circumstances.

Disclaimer
Any similarity to actual people or places is purely coincidental, as names and places were altered to protect the confidentiality of our clients and professional associates.

Cover Design: Bill Johnson
First Edition
17 18 19 20 — 9 8 7 6 5 4 3 2 1
Printed in the United States of America

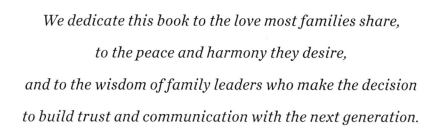

We dedicate this book to the love most families share,

to the peace and harmony they desire,

and to the wisdom of family leaders who make the decision

to build trust and communication with the next generation.

Acknowledgments

To our families—

It is with grateful hearts and deep humility that we acknowledge the support and wisdom we have been given by so many caring and loving families over the past fifty-two years. It is through your wisdom, your willingness to trust us with your private conversations, and your commitment to family harmony and unity that we are able to share this book with you.

We also express our thanks to the original 2,500 families surveyed who first shared your families' experiences and results, and those surveyed since. We appreciate your willingness to be open to learn, grow, and overcome the reluctance and discomfort change can create. You enabled us to develop and refine our process through trial and error.

To **The Executive Committee (TEC) International**, and especially to **Bill Williams**, the Executive Director and Roy's T.E.C. mates—You were greatly responsible for Roy's early business success and provided valuable guidance.

Our grateful thanks to the many friends, clients, trusted supporters, and advisors who contributed their insight and experience to the book in so many ways. You also became part of the team. Without you, this book would lack its richness.

Thank you also to Dick Boyd, David Boyd, Pete Coors, Joe Harper, Jose Higueras, Glen Holden, and Art and Sarah Ludwick.

A heartfelt thank you to Ed Halbach, Professor Emeritus, UC Berkeley School of Law, and his dear wife of sixty-five years, Janet B. Halbach, who have been a consistent source of wisdom. Ed passed away in June 2017 shortly after sending us his endorsement for this book. We will miss you, Ed.

A big thank you to Victor Preisser for your genius in developing the algorithms for the 10-Question Quiz and the Family Readiness Assessment survey that indicates the core issues for families.

Grateful thanks to Diana Williams, counselor of the first rank, wise sounding board, trusted partner, provider of inexhaustible editing contributions, and one who continually demonstrated the very essence of this book; the embodiment of a unified and loving family. Diana passed away in March 2017. She was truly the wind beneath Roy's wings for fifty-nine years.

Our thanks to the members of **our world-class coaching team** who have contributed your invaluable expert experience and training and meaningfully added to the book's depth and relevance. A very special thanks to Amy Castoro, Peter Yaholkovsky, Susan Staker, Joel and Judy Kimmel, and Debbie Daniels. Thanks also to Mike Allen, a talented attorney, for your extraordinary analysis regarding inconsistencies in logic and language.

Likewise to Marion MacGillivray, whose determination and subtle insistence and passion for the work we do have significantly contributed to and orchestrated the compilation of this work with grace and humor. Marion has been our primary driver in getting the new book completed and sent to our publisher.

Much gratitude to Anne Marie Glenn Sanchez for your unique organization skills, for your stalwart belief in our work, and for being a champion of consistency in our processes.

We are grateful to all for your contributions!

Contents

Tables, Charts, and Questionnaires

Foreword

This wise book by Roy Williams and Amy Castoro takes the preparing heirs conversation to a new level of understanding and
action with new stories and current insights for today's readers.
This book includes the benefit of many additional years of field
studies with families (and their trusted advisors) to ensure their
legacies endure. As a true test of time, the steps highlighted that
have brought many families unity and harmony, remain true to
Roy's original vision.

Roy's and Amy's insight into family dynamics and wealth transition is a powerful force reversing the trend of the 70 percent
failure rate. Their work enables families to cultivate the family
values that have driven us to reach the level of success we enjoy,
and then to pass them on to our next generations. Without a clear
sense of who they are, what makes them who they are, the next
generations are at risk of being adrift in the vicissitudes of wealth.
Regrettably I have seen this play out all too often.

Many of us have developed a family vision, and in some cases an
organization to take care of the family wealth. Probably not unlike
your situation, our family business is becoming more complicated
as we transition to the next generations.

Though our financial advisors, attorneys and accountants have
taken the necessary steps to protect our wealth and to ensure
that it will transfer according to our plans, I chose to proactively
prepare my family members to be prepared to receive the wealth.
The Williams Group teaches the family tried and tested trust and
communication skills, identifies with the family the values the
family holds in common, and with the family develops the long-
term purpose/mission of the family. We have discovered the true
wealth of the family is the values the family holds, and enduring
relationships.

Roy and Amy point to the essence of how to transfer family values and how to retain family unity and harmony. How to have the

family drive the wealth versus the wealth drive the family. Your family values are key, and mining those from the rich history of your family is the gift you can give your next generations. It is the values we live by that are the best indicators of success. Through them we can find our purpose, the hidden force behind the every day decisions and actions you and your next generation are taking now, that will impact their future.

Through the work of The Williams Group families learn the essential skills of how to build trust with one another, move beyond the past and see new ways of building relationships, foster direction, purpose and involvement for individual family members, and for the family as a unit. Family is placed front and center. The family learns the necessary skills required to work together as a high performing team, turn conflict into a generative way forward, and take accountability for the responsibilities of their family unity and wealth. These skills build confidence, competence, and the necessary ambition in the next generation so they can step up to the plate and impact their world in meaningful ways.

For Roy, Amy and their team, the ROI is when a family comes together and impacts the world in ways that reflect their own values and as a result makes the world a better place.

—**Pete Coors**
Chairman, Coors Brewing Corporation

Preface

On The Shoulders of Giants

Sir Isaac Newton (1676) is quoted as saying, "If I have seen further, it has been by standing on the shoulders of giants."

The following giants had a huge impact on me, during my life and early career, and it is with gratitude that I clearly remember and am forever grateful to their generosity in sharing their insights about the estate planning and finance industry. They allowed me to stand on their shoulders--enabling me to see further.

It was 1963, and I was fresh out of being released by the San Francisco 49ers due to a torn-up knee, I had a wife, three sons, and I needed a job to support them. Fortunately, during those first six months, I met some industry giants. Their advice to me was to focus on *solving problems*, not selling products. I asked them, "What problems; how do I learn about them?"

They suggested I attend courses at the USC Tax Institute, The Miami Tax Institute, and The Practicing Law Institute of Dallas. I did so, and met other giants in the field, such as Professor Ed Halbach, the Dean at University of California Law School; Professor A. James Casner at Harvard, and many more, including Mike Allen, an ACTEC member in Tyler, Texas. I learned that most wills, trusts and estate plans focused solely on tax-reduction, wealth preservation and how best to govern the assets that would be gifted to the next generations. Certainly these financial aspects are very important. And we have come to know that they cannot be the sole focus of estate planning and wealth transfer.

Focusing on the evident and much publicized family problems that transpired after financial assets were transferred helped me recognize the 70 percent failure rate, exemplified by the rags-to-riches-to-rags stories that were and continue to be so pervasive. Consider the recent coup attempt by the Buss brothers to gain control of the Lakers over their sister, or the astronomical request for fees of $100M by the executors of Leona Helmsley's estate, resulting in the NY attorney general stepping in with the decision that these fees were egregious, and the multitude of other wealthy family feuds, past and present.

I love the well-known quote, "The definition of insanity is continuing to do the same thing over and over again and expecting different results." I relate this to families continuing to focus solely on tax reduction, governance, and wealth preservation and expecting the rags-to-riches-to-rags issues to disappear.

Clients repeatedly asked me how to address the concerns they had about their heirs. How could they successfully transfer their wealth to their children and avoid the wealth destroying their relationships and wellbeing? These concerns needed to be addressed. (Remember my original mentors' advice about solving problems?)

What was causing the 70 percent failure-rate problem in wealth transition? I went back to my friendly giants and asked this question. They were unable to identify the source of the problem. The evidence of the problem was that many families ended up in disputes that destroyed the family unity and often resulted in expensive litigation.

I set out on a quest to understand the origins of this problem by interviewing professors from the leading law and accounting schools, leaders of the top business schools, MBA's, lawyers, and accountants, all whom I knew and respected. No one could give me the answers I was looking for. They were unable to adequately identify the root cause of the problem. I came to understand that professional financial advisors and estate planners are well educated and trained and do a credible job of wealth preservation, governance, and taxation reduction. Less than 5 percent of failed wealth-transition plans are attributable to these three issues.

One morning I awoke at 3 a.m. with the thought, "Why not ask the clients?" TEC (The Executive Committee) International of which I was a member, allowed me to talk to 1,000 of their members, as a resource. I took this as an opportunity to interview them. They, in turn, introduced me to people they knew in their communities who had lost their family wealth. Twenty years later, and more than 2,500 people interviewed, I had the insight into the problem of why there was a 70 percent failure rate at the post-transition level.

The problem became clearer - the breakdowns resulted from the focus being limited solely to the financial assets being transferred *and the unity and harmony of the family itself being ignored; which was showing up as the most important and critical asset.* Without a strong foundation of family unity, the estate plans were only as good as the paper they were written on. There are main drivers of wealth transfer failure as it relates to family dynamics - 60 percent of the time, lack of trust was at the core of breakdowns–without trust, there was no possibility for authentic communication. To address the 70 percent failure rate, we had to find a way to solve the trust and communication breakdowns. Once we addressed these breakdowns, we would be able to address the other two core issues – the 25 percent unprepared heirs issue, and the 10 percent lack of a family wealth mission.

Over the next 20 years, we made more mistakes than God should allow, and we learned. Thanks to more giants in various fields... Fernando Flores, Richard Heckler, many of our coaches, and just to name a few, Amy Castoro, Peter Yaholkovsky, Joel Kimmel, Sue Staker, Debbie Daniels, and numerous others in various fields...They've helped us in so many ways to understand and develop a program to address the three core issues.

Out of this learning we developed The Williams Group Process™, with a high success rate and many families endorsing our work. The families who work with us are living testimony that what we are doing and sharing with others works. We are regularly invited back to check in on how well their learning has been retained, or as the family expands, or to provide support through a particular situation. It is my sincere hope that what you discover and embrace from reading this book will be the key to you and your family successfully passing the baton and the wealth you have created will be a force for good in your family and the world.

—Roy Williams

Introduction to Bridging Generations

Amy A. Castoro

Every year, hundreds of books are published on wealth transfer, estate planning, and family business leadership. And each year, the number of organizations, services, and educational outlets dedicated to serving the ultra-wealthy continues to grow. We see the number of family offices and multifamily offices increasing.

The largest transfer of wealth in the history of capitalism is under way, and it is startling how few people are addressing the core issues that are proven indicators of successful transfer, family harmony, and unity. If you are looking for quick fixes, strategies, and structure to perpetuate wealth, you will not find it here. What this book will do, though, is ask you the tough questions that set the course of deeper inquiry. It will ignite your curiosity about what it means to be a family and to define wealth, the purpose of your wealth, and the legacy you are building for your lineage. It is not until these foundational questions are answered that a strong infrastructure of a sustainable estate transition plan and legacy can be built.

One of Roy's favorite quotes is, "The two most important days in your life are the day you are born and the day you find out why." This book is a tribute to those words in the most fundamental way. It speaks to the truth of purpose. Many people ask the question, "How much should I pass on to my heirs, and when?" Roy's driving purpose for most of his life has been to educate families that they are asking the wrong question. As you will read in the pages that follow, the responsibility of significant wealth is not just wrought with opportunities; all too often, it is typified by disastrous consequences for the family. Day after day, the media report on yet another example of an affluent family whose legacy has ended up in family disputes or in litigation among family members because of a lack of trust.

As the baton of the family business and wealth is passed, millennials today find themselves stepping into larger, more complex organizations in a marketplace characterized by swiftly changing global forces. Their concerns are about how to professionalize the organization, how to build larger and more effective teams, how to navigate the immense information available to them through the Internet, and ultimately how to decipher what and whom they can trust.

Many millennials are growing up with a background of abundance, as opposed to the mood of scarcity that typified the economic pressures of their parents' generation. When we ask millennials from high-net-worth families today what they are striving for, they don't say, "I want to be a millionaire." They say, "I want to be a billionaire."

And they want to do it on their terms. Fortunately, the traits of this generation encompass many of the qualities that are fundamental to building trust and high-performing family teams, such as transparency, collaboration, work/family balance, and learning. The challenge is bridging the gap between the generational belief systems.

Roy's quest has been to demonstrate that it is possible to pass on wealth in ways that breed family harmony and unity and allow families to thrive for generations. Learning the skills of building and repairing trust enables conversations and actions to emerge that create deep and long-lasting relationships and prosperity.

This book is a manifestation of our commitment to building social practices that fan the early embers of care and love in a family and the family business. Inside these pages are fundamental, practical, and attainable steps a family can take to avoid the documented 70 percent failure rate.

Often referred to as the Dean of Post-Transition Wealth Transfer (Roy demurs and states that it is The Williams Group coaches who are so skilled in transforming families), Roy and I have written this book to provide unique insights that speak to the timeless language of trust, communication, and teamwork. It is predicated on the fact that the skills of trust and communication can be learned, and the best platform for that learning are the very important and often sidestepped conversations within a family.

This book offers specific examples gleaned from The Williams Group's fifty-two years of working with affluent families and the lessons learned. It offers attainable and pragmatic steps every family can take as a path to deepen trust and sharpen communication skills to ensure that they navigate wealth transition successfully.

Research shows that, when followed, legal, tax, and governance guidelines can ensure that assets transition smoothly. Whether or not the assets unify or divide the family and/or remain within control of the inheriting generation is very much dependent on three major factors measured in the ground-breaking field studies Roy conducted with more than 2,500 wealthy families. These studies form the foundation for the claims in this book, and they continue to be validated by current studies.

If you are the head of a family, or a trusted advisor to one, you will find this book refreshingly easy to read. The pragmatic wisdom we share will provide you the steady footing necessary to navigate the fragile yet powerful force of a united family.

Chapter 1 examines the role of family values, unity, and harmony in a successful wealth transfer.

In chapter 2, we discuss the trends in and impact of wealth transfer and the differences between generations.

Chapter 3 looks more closely at the implications of the field study and provides pragmatic questions you can ask yourself to reveal new ways to address the core aspects of successful wealth transfers and succession. It also contains a 10-Question Quiz developed by The Williams Group, which you can take to obtain a quick assessment of your family's readiness for a successful wealth transfer and succession.

Chapter 4 provides the first of five steps, The Williams Group road map to a successful wealth transition, and information on The Williams Group 50-Question Survey.

Chapter 5 offers the second "how to" step to secure your financial and family wealth by unifying your family. Family meetings are covered in depth.

The third step in chapter 6 identifies wealth-transition deficiencies with tried and tested solutions to turn them into an action plan for success.

The fourth and fifth steps to prepare the family are clearly delineated in chapters 7 and 8. They include the eight levels of competence, as well as a 10-question survey for family leaders and another survey for family members to assess their self-preparedness and responsibilities for successful wealth transfers and succession.

Chapter 9 explores formal structures such as a family council, a family board, or a family office as a means to support the relationships at the intersection of family members, ownership, and the family business.

Chapter 10 discusses the importance of the family leading the wealth, as opposed to the wealth leading the family, and provides a summary of the book.

1

Will Your Wealth Transfer Unify or Divide Your Family?

"I tell college students, when you get to be my age you will be successful if the people who you hope to have love you do love you."

—**Warren Buffett**

What Is Wealth?

Most people define wealth as a list of assets, including money, stocks, bonds, business assets, real estate, commercial and personal property, and intellectual property.

The Williams Group and many families we work with define wealth as follows:

> Wealth encompasses all forms of family assets and resources: money, assets, stocks, bonds, real estate, commercial and personal property, intellectual property, and business interests,

as well as the family name and reputation. It also includes the family history; experience and education; the intellectual, social, and networking capacity of all family members, including spouses; and most importantly, the existing asset of the entire family itself, children and spouses, grandchildren and spouses, adopted children and stepchildren—and the family values, unity, and harmony.

Family unity and harmony are perhaps the most powerful components necessary for long-term wealth, yet family values, unity, and harmony are frequently not considered as part of the family's net worth.

The reality is that tangible financial assets, coupled with relatively secure strategy and structure for the transfer of the assets, do not guarantee that the family will prosper into the future. This has motivated successful families to focus proactively on family values and on development of family unity and harmony to sustain growth and development of the family legacy.

This book is based on our understanding that there are two distinct and interdependent aspects of legacy: (1) financial assets and (2) family unity and harmony. To ensure a successful transfer of assets from one generation to the next, the family is called to address the financial and the family unity aspects proactively by giving them both the time, energy, and attention they require and deserve. Historically, the aspect that has received the most attention is the creation and transfer of financial assets.

Well-documented evidence indicates that the greatest threat to successful wealth transfer lies within a poorly prepared family prior to the transfer taking place. It is startling to compare how much time and money are spent on preparing for a transfer of the financial assets with how little time and money are spent on preparing the beneficiaries to receive the assets, manage the wealth, and secure the family unity.

This book provides the tools and steps you can take now to prepare and protect your family from the catastrophic impact wealth can have on an unprepared family.

Proactively preparing family members requires resolving breakdowns in communication, identifying family values, developing a family wealth mission/purpose statement, aligning estate plans with the family wealth mission/purpose, identifying the family's needs and roles, developing qualification and performance standards, and preparing family members who choose to fill the roles according to their interests and passions.

The First Decision: Who Is Family?

Families decide on their own definition of family. In addition to the family leaders, the family fabric can be woven with second, third and fourth generations and their spouses and adopted children as well as stepchildren.

As the leader of your family, your legacy ultimately depends on your decision to learn, along with your entire family, the tools of successful families who have gone before. Financial advisors, estate planners, attorneys, or family members who factor in the family's preparedness, succession plans, and unity into the preservation of wealth equation will better serve the family.

Well-documented evidence indicates that the greatest threat to successful wealth transfer lies within a poorly prepared family prior to the transfer taking place.

The father of a large family who was confronting the challenge of passing along his wealth said, "I have entertained thoughts of simply giving it all away to a good cause. My children are all so entitled. It has been a profound sense of disappointment to me." Because he grew up in a family of eight who subsisted on powdered milk and hand-me-down clothing, he was committed to providing a better life and more opportunity for his own children. He possessed an above-average facility for numbers, a fearlessness toward risk taking, very high energy, and unbridled ambition: an excellent recipe for success.

While he was generating his wealth, the possibility that it

could destroy his family was the furthest thought from his mind. His commitment to creating a better life financially for his family blinded him to the impact that the wealth, without family connection, family values, and a family wealth mission/purpose, could have on unprepared family members. He had also been blind to the impact that putting money, business, and work before his family would have on his children.

This dad's absence, as he worked constantly and determinedly to build his empire, resulted in entitled children who had a distant relationship with their father. They went to him only when they needed something. Their lives were adrift without direction or purpose in a sea of opportunity and affluence. As his wealth grew, the need to control the increasing complexity of his company and his estate demanded all his focus. Their family life suffered.

Years passed, and the inevitable awareness of mortality loomed on the horizon. Recognizing the need for a successor conflicted with letting go of control. The pressure mounted and expressed itself through longer hours at work, less connection with family, and family members being unprepared for succession and wealth transfer. His children came to believe that money and business were higher priorities for him than they were.

As the number of wealthy families increases, along with the size of their portfolios and the unprecedented avalanche of wealth transfer begins as baby boomers retire, this story becomes more common today than ever. Without preparation, the consequence to families and society can be devastating. It is likely an underestimate that 70 percent of families are unprepared and unlikely to transfer their wealth successfully, according to various experts.[1] It is no surprise to us when

He had also been blind to the impact that putting money, business, and work before his family would have on his children.

---

1. Richard Beckhard and W. Gibb Dyer, "Managing Continuity in the Family-Owned Business," *Organizational Dynamics*, Summer 1983, AMA, p.5. At that time, Beckhard was an adjunct professor of management at the Alfred P. Sloane School of Management at MIT. Also from "The New Wealth of Nations," *The Economist* (June 16, 2001), 3ff.

the head of a family says, "I would give it all away if it means I can have my family back."

The good news is that once the breakdowns are identified, the causes can be addressed. Working with affluent families for more than fifty-two years and our extensive research tell us that it is possible to unite families to become high-performing family teams and preserve both financial assets and the family unity generationally.

Successful transfers of wealth typically rely on proactive, long-range strategy and structure planning with attorneys, accountants, and financial, tax, and insurance advisors, who develop the necessary plans for tax reduction, wealth preservation, and transfer of the financial assets. These professionals are mostly successful at accomplishing these tasks.

Traditionally, addressing financial assets and estate planning was considered sufficient. But a single-family meeting to deliver instructions no longer works, especially when many competent adult family members are involved. Advisors are no longer able to limit their focus to the technical structure of wealth; they must think through how things will play out in reality. Then they must recommend additional professional services to address any issues of concern that fall outside their domain.

However, as far back as the Prodigal Son, *the real indicator of successful wealth transfer and succession lies within the family itself.* It is essential to develop trust, communication, and unity of the family first to ensure a successful transfer of wealth, with the wealth remaining under control of the current family members and future generations.

It has been said that the definition of insanity is doing the same

Advisors are no longer able to limit their focus to the technical structure of wealth; they must think through how things will play out in reality.

thing over and over again and expecting different results. So if a wealth-transfer plan isn't working, it's time to try a new approach.

The Williams Group's Definition of a Successful Wealth Transfer

A successful transfer of assets constitutes a proactive, carefully considered, planned strategy and structure covering the financial assets, combined with a cohesive robust process that includes all family members and results in future generations retaining the family's financial assets while remaining a unified family.

In a successful transfer, the next generations have been prepared proactively to receive the assets through the process of developing trust and effective communication skills, identifying individual aspirations, co-creating family values, developing an agreed-on family wealth mission, aligning the estate plan with the family wealth mission, identifying the needs that require roles to be filled and developed by the entire family and team, and establishing qualification and performance standards for those roles. These families recognize the most important asset a family has is family unity and harmony. When family unity is destroyed, all can be lost.

Causes of the 70% Failure Rate in Estate Transitions

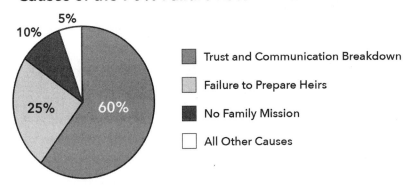

Figure 1-1: As stated earlier, the origins of the 70 percent failure rate in estate transitions have been found to lie within the family itself. By the same token, the 30 percent success rate lies within the family itself.

The breakdown of trust and communication within the family is weighted at 60 percent. Heirs being unprepared to be accountable and responsible is weighted at 25 percent. The lack of a purpose/mission for the wealth is weighted at 10 percent.

We address these issues throughout this book and provide you with five steps to a successful wealth transfer and succession. The chapters highlight the skills and actions you can take today to prepare your family. We have included three different 10-Question Quizzes in chapters 3, 7, and 8 that can help you assess where you and your family members are in relationship to a successful wealth transfer and succession.

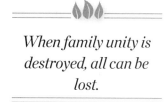

When family unity is destroyed, all can be lost.

As a family leader, how assured are you that all the wealth you have worked so hard to create will be a force for good in your family, engendering family unity and harmony, and not its demise?

If you will succeed your parents, how certain are you and the rest of your family that you have the necessary skills to ensure that your generation and the next will successfully navigate the transfer? As you can see from the statistics, regrettably, the odds are not in your favor.

We wrote this book for four general categories of people:

- First-generation wealth creators

- The more tenured wealthy, those with so-called "old money"

- A successor to a wealth creator

- A financial advisor, banker, estate planner, or attorney, who cares deeply about the families you work with

Let's take a look at each category.

1. First-generation wealth creators—Two-thirds of the world's wealthiest people fall into this category. If you are one of them, this may be the first time you are involved in family wealth succession planning. You are likely finding yourself confronted by the challenges of learning how to transfer the wealth you have generated to future generations successfully.

Generating wealth requires one set of skills, while transferring that wealth requires another. Both can be learned. If the landscape of succession is new to you, what is required is an awareness of what to pay attention to, development of the necessary new skills, and a commitment to implementation. You have already achieved the necessary skills in the domain of financial wealth creation. As your family grows in number and maturity, it is insufficient to limit your focus on the aspect of creating wealth. You are now called to lead, be a role model, educate, and prepare your family for how to handle this wealth in ways that carry forth the central values you and your family hold, to ensure family unity across the generations.

2. The more tenured wealthy, those with so-called "old money"—If this describes you, you might find yourself confronted by more challenging wealth transitions than your predecessors as the family continues to grow in number and complexity. The call for a stronger sense of continuity of the family values, wealth, and unity into the next generations is more present than ever before as the world also becomes increasingly complex and changes with increasing velocity. Keeping a larger family informed and connected, and establishing structures for that communication and coordination are essential.

Generating wealth requires one set of skills, while transferring that wealth requires another.

3. A successor to a wealth creator—If you are in this category, being aware of the 70 percent failure rate and the reality that the major challenges lie within the family members, you might feel the responsibility and obligation to carry the gift forward by being prepared for the roles that will be required and ensuring that the pitfalls of family dissention do not happen on your watch.

4. A financial advisor, banker, estate planner, or attorney who cares deeply about the families you work with—You are probably equally concerned about the 70 percent failure rate. Perhaps you even see some of the early signs of poor communication, mistrust, and lack of purpose beginning to surface. Your commitment to support your clients' need to be successful in their wealth transition may be compelling you to ask the question of how to support the family as a unified whole. When they succeed, you have succeeded in fulfilling your mandate.

Many define a successful wealth transfer and succession as "wealth remaining under the control of the beneficiaries." If the asset ownership changes form (e.g., the business is sold and the family financial assets are converted to cash or other forms of value), that is a *reformatting* of wealth, not a measure of success or failure. The same is true when the beneficiary redistributes his or her wealth as voluntary, informed philanthropic decisions. Conversely, if when following the wealth transfer the beneficiaries lose control of their wealth through foolish expenditure, bad investments, mismanagement, inattention, incompetence, family disharmony, feuding, litigation, or other causes within their control, then the transfer of assets is classified as *unsuccessful.*

Here are two fundamental questions the heads of families, financial advisors, and family members are faced with: How can the family be prepared to ensure that the wealth transfer and succession will be successful in terms of both financial assets and family unity? We know what to do with respect to the financial assets, but what do we need to do to preserve and deepen family unity and harmony?

Most people reading a book about family wealth transfer and succession might answer those questions with a fair amount of confidence, given the planning they have done with their accountants, attorneys, and tax, insurance, and financial advisors. Others, being aware of the frequency of family feuds, will wonder if the succession planning they have done will prevent further feuding and litigation from happening in their family.

This book provides the overview, steps, and processes to develop and strengthen family unity so families can leave a legacy that will bring peace and prosperity to the next generations.

The Williams Group has worked with affluent families for more than fifty-two years. We have conducted extensive field studies with more than 2,500 families and then added 1,000 more families who have successfully transferred their assets, as well as families who have experienced failure in the transfer of assets. Sadly, again, this ratio has historically been widely recognized as 30 percent success and 70 percent failure. This is known internationally as "shirtsleeves-to-shirtsleeves in three generations," "rice bowl to rice bowl in three generations," or "clogs to clogs…" The Chinese have a saying, *"Fu bu guo san dai,"* which means "Wealth never survives three generations."

How can the family be prepared to ensure that the wealth transfer and succession will be successful in terms of both financial assets and family unity?

As a result of our studies and our work with affluent families, we have developed tools and processes to help families succeed in transferring both their financial and family assets to future generations.[2]

Throughout this book, you will find valuable steps and tools for developing trust, engaging in meaningful conversations productively, and setting your family up for success.

Chapter 1 Summary

Two-thirds of all wealth transfers are from first-generation wealth creators. As far back as the Prodigal Son, the heads of families have passed their assets onto the next generation with little or no preparation. Sometimes that works. But evidence of it not working is the 70 percent failure rate of wealth transitions, which resulted in the "shirtsleeves-to-shirtsleeves in three generations" phe-

---

2. Appendix 1 details the research for those who would like to understand the investigative process further.

nomenon. This is the norm, not the exception.

The significant role that the family plays in the 70 percent failure rate of wealth transitions needs to be addressed within the family. This failure rate results primarily from the lack of proactively preparing family members. Through research with affluent families, we have identified that a breakdown of trust and communication within the family is weighted 60 percent. Heirs being unprepared to be accountable and responsible is weighted 25 percent. And the lack of a purpose/mission for the wealth is weighted 10 percent.

To achieve family unity requires well-thought-out tools and processes. The family needs to decide who is considered family. Family can include simply the blood line, or adopted children, spouses, etc. The important thing is it is a conversation within the family, about the family.

Proactively preparing family members requires resolving breakdowns in communication, identifying family values, developing a family wealth mission/purpose statement, aligning estate plans with the family wealth mission/purpose, establishing individual aspirations, identifying the needs and roles the family has, developing qualification and performance standards, and preparing family members who choose to fulfill those roles according to their interests and passions.

Once the breakdowns are identified, they can be addressed. The Williams Group has developed a robust and proven process and tools that are provided throughout this book to unite families.

The goal is to create high-performing family teams, preserve the financial assets, and develop family unity intergenerationally.

CHAPTER

2

Wealth-Transfer Trends— "Passing the Buck"

"How did you go bankrupt? Gradually, then suddenly."

—**Ernest Hemingway,** *The Sun Also Rises*

"In the past, parents didn't worry very much about the effects of wealth on their children," says Virginia Esposito, founding president of the National Center for Family Philanthropy. "When it was time to pass on to the next generation, then that's what you did without much thinking about it."

The high-net-worth family of today has become more complex and diverse. The concept of *family* is continually evolving. As a result of longer life spans, access to good health care, and the frequency of multiple marriages, we are becoming a nation with many diverse and blended families. These changing family structures, which often include the co-existence of multiple generations of immediate and extended family members, require new ways of interacting, the development of new relationships, and a higher skill level of communication. People being people, blending families is more likely to increase the complexity of wealth transitions with potential for more disagreements over the assets. This represents a significant risk to wealth transfer. On top of that, the economic and social changes that have happened in recent history have had a profound impact on how people's values and interpretations are formed.

With the aging of the silent generation (born between 1925 and 1937) and baby boomers (born between 1946 and 1964), who will significantly shape the future wealth of younger generations through substantial bequests, it is predicted that over the next several decades, the largest and wealthiest generations in US history will transfer approximately $30 trillion in assets to their Gen X (born between 1965 and 1980) and millennial children (born between 1981 and 1997) and their grandchildren and great-grandchildren—generation Z/digital natives (born after 1994.) Dates are approximate.

The cultural, social, and economic events that shaped each of these generations also shapes their values. Creating an understanding of how historical events impact each generation helps build a bridge to their experience. We begin with the silent generation, which was plagued by war and economic instability due to the Great Depression (1929–39) and then World War II. At the same time, this generation enjoyed the advent of television and motion pictures with sound and witnessed America surpassing its previous economic status and becoming a global superpower. This status came about with the birth of computers, the Internet,

The cultural, social, and economic events that shaped each of these generations also shapes their values.

GENERATIC

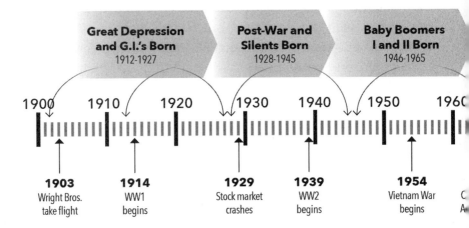

iPods, cell phones, entrepreneurship, workaholics, networking, and the Great Recession, which began in 2008.

Sandwiched between the silent generation and the digital native generation, the United States was involved in numerous wars: World War II, Korea, Vietnam, Afghanistan, Iraq, Persian Gulf, Kosovo, and the war on ISI/ISIS. Today the country is fighting day-to-day terrorism by radical Islamic groups worldwide. The civil rights, the women's, girls', and environmental movements grew during these times.

During this time span, the American generations were influenced by McCarthyism, when many citizens lived in fear of being accused of being communists; the assassinations of President Kennedy, Robert Kennedy, and Martin Luther King, Jr.; and the resignation of President Nixon. These very tumultuous political times were followed by Presidents Ford and Carter, Reaganomics, the Bush years, and the appointment of Obama, the first black president of the United States.

As time progressed, the rights of children and their welfare were increasingly recognized. According to the Library of Con-

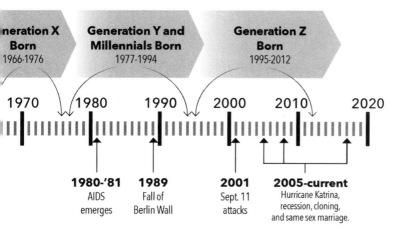

gress[3] up until the late nineteenth century, children were largely considered property and economic assets. The 1924 UN Declaration of the Rights of the Child (DRC), the 1989 Convention on the Rights of the Child (CRC), and legal instruments on children's rights were developed with the intent to protect all aspects of a child's life up to the age of eighteen. Today labor laws protect millennials with respect to how the information they post on social media can be used in the hiring process.

The chart shown above represents the historical events and impact on generations. Though there is consensus on a general time period for American generations, different sources use varying dates to mark their beginning and ending years.

Parenting styles during these years emerged from the era of the authoritarian parenting style, when children were controlled by fear and love—"seen but not heard"—to various other parenting styles. One phenomenon that emerged was "latchkey" children, who were loved but frequently left to their own devices because both parents' incomes were needed to support the family. Other

3. "Children's Rights: International Laws," Library of Congress website, http://www.loc.gov/law/help/child-rights/international-law.php.

parenting styles that emerged include permissive parenting, un-involved parenting, hovering parenting, a consistent 20 percent faith-based parenting, and everything in between.

All the above factors are powerful influences of generational effects on the generations who will be passing on their wealth and the recipients.

Today there are roughly 10.8 million millennial households[4] with children. According to an analysis of new US Census Bureau data[5], millennials now compose the largest share of the American workforce. They are also becoming the largest demographic that represents parents. Most millennial parents were slower to mature and had children later than previous generations, want/need to be a two-career family, are entrepreneurs, share the raising of their children, and provide home care as a team. They want to be more involved than baby boomers, for whom "parenting" wasn't even yet a verb, and they want to hover less than those "helicopter" moms of Gen X.

Just as they are natural networkers and believe in a diverse portfolio of social media accounts, millennials have grown up Googling everything, checking feedback, and using this information to make up their own minds. They incorporate aspects of various child-raising philosophies based on child development, their Google findings, and psychological understanding. They have high hopes for their children and invest their time and energy, pouring themselves fully into their families' futures.

Today there are roughly 10.8 million millennial households with children.

The millennials and digital natives who will inherit the majority of the wealth transfer have been raised to be independent in their thinking and do not question whether they will be heard or not. They definitely intend to have their say and be heard.

4. "Why A 'One-Size-Fits-All' Approach No Longer Works For Millennial Employees", Wes Gay, www.forbes.com, 10/26/2016, https://www.forbes.com/sites/wesgay/2016/10/10/older-millennials/2/#1ddc17d7eb9b.
5. "Millennials Outnumber Baby Boomers and Are Far More Diverse, Census Bureau Reports," US Census Bureau website, June 25, 2016, https://www.census.gov/newsroom/press-releases/2015/cb15-113.html.

In this information age, millennials' sociocultural environment has inflated to a size larger than any previous generation—they are truly global citizens. They readily share information (sometimes too much), and information travels rapidly through their vast communication networks. They are sophisticated in their global concerns, are less likely to follow directions blindly, and appear to be devoid of hierarchy and traditional Industrial Age rules. They are the "now" generation. Instant gratification comes in the form of next day deliveries for anything they can imagine, relationships formed with a swipe left or right and can download an entire series without having to wait a week to catch the next episode.

Very frequently, they desire to make a meaningful contribution in the world. Perhaps the most significant difference among these generations is that millennials of means only know abundance. Many have never known what it is like to worry about making a mortgage payment, keeping a job, bouncing checks, or paying for school.

The burning question is this: Given this diverse group of values, what can those transferring wealth do to ensure that the legacy they want to leave is successfully transferred without resulting in family dissention?

One of the inherent differences between the generations transferring their wealth and the recipient generations is that the latter desire open, honest communication and collaboration.

Traditionally, Mom and Dad would work with an attorney and other advisors to decide how the wealth would be distributed. Their wills included their directives, and the expectation was that their wishes would be carried out. Recurrently, this very lack of transparency creates the largest degree of cordial hypocrisy and breeds

The millennials and digital natives who will inherit the majority of the wealth transfer have been raised to be independent in their thinking and do not question whether they will be heard or not.

the most dangerous type of mood—a mood of resentment. If the next generation does not understand the values that shaped the decisions Mom and Dad have made, they are left with making interpretations from legal documents, as opposed to knowing the reasons based on discussions held with the entire family.

Today, in families of significant wealth, the complexity of distribution and constantly changing legal and tax strategies clearly indicate a collectively agreed-upon succession plan is necessary. Successful wealth transfers require intentional, proactive planning prior to the wealth transfer taking place. This needs to involve both the estate planners, who will advise on the structure and strategy for the legal, tax-reduction, and governance aspects, and the *entire* family, and requires preparing the heirs for their roles based on agreed family values and a co-created family wealth mission for how to handle the wealth in the future. When you've worked hard to build your legacy, it makes total sense to take the necessary steps to ensure that it will last for generations.

The Impact of Transferred Wealth on Unprepared Heirs

Our studies indicate that leaders of families share a similar set of questions and concerns regarding the potential impact wealth may have on their children and grandchildren. They are also concerned about whether the family's values underlying the accumulation of wealth will be transmitted along with the wealth and reflected in how the wealth is used.

Numerous wealth inheritors have been impacted in a positive way; they have embraced their parents' values and family wealth mission/purpose, followed in their parents' footsteps, and are committed to worthy causes. At the same time, we hear many stories about wealthy children who appear to be without direction, have little or no interest in doing good in the world, and instead appear to be overly entitled and self-indulgent. Some revel in negative publicity, become spendthrifts, develop addictions, get involved in legal incidents, and gain notoriety.

One of the saddest stories we have heard about the unsuccessful transfer of family wealth involved a root issue of disengagement and the belief that the wealth was a burden. A law firm's senior partner shared with us the story of a young man whose father was very successful in real estate. His father died unexpectedly and at age thirty-five, without any preparation, the son received his father's sizable estate. The estate amounted to $110 million, plus the equivalent of a square city block of commercial real estate.

Three years later, at age thirty-eight, the son committed suicide. The note he left was a sad commentary. He had lost the "I can hardly wait" aspect of life. In the note, he said that most people have times when they could hardly wait for a weekend to do something. He could do anything he wanted whenever he wanted; there was nothing to wait for. He had no wife and no children. He had access to women, friends, travel, cars–anything he wanted–yet he did not know if the friends were friends because of who he was or because he was rich. He had no purpose, felt alone, and thought he had nothing worth living for.

Where was the family unity for this young man? At age thirty-five, why was he unprepared to receive and manage this wealth? Obviously, there are numerous factors that determine outcomes. One factor we have witnessed over the years that negatively impacts the direction of family members is lack of preparation.

The following table provides an objective summary of some parents' apprehensions regarding the impact their current wealth and the wealth they plan to transfer to their children may have on them. Operating in the background of these concerns are the fundamental values of the family that are explicitly or invisibly shaping the parents' and children's actions and outcomes. The majority of these concerns can be addressed through parental modeling and proactively preparing the next generations.

The following chart from US Trust Survey reveals what worries affluent parents most about the effect of wealth on their children.[6]

What worries affluent parents most about the effect of wealth on their children	Percent who are worried
Too much emphasis on material things	60 percent
Naive about the value of money	55 percent
Spend beyond their means	52 percent
Have their initiative ruined by affluence	50 percent
Not do as well financially as parent would like	49 percent
Not do as well financially as parent did	44 percent
Hard time taking financial responsibility	42 percent
Resented because of their affluence	36 percent
Suffer from parental absences	35 percent
Date or marry someone who wants affluence	34 percent
Limited exposure to non-affluent people	33 percent
Think they have big shoes to fill and that they will fail	18 percent

An additional impact of unprepared heirs that has been evidenced in the last decade, and that concerns financial advisors, heads of families, and family members, is that the heirs change financial advisors. "Studies regularly show that when wealth passes to another generation, in the majority of cases, the heirs change financial advisors," --Gauthier Vincent, head of Deloitte's US Wealth Management practice.[7]

The majority of these concerns can be addressed through parental modeling and proactively preparing the next generations.

6. US Trust Survey of Affluent Americans XIX, December 2000.
7. Gauthier Vincent, head of Deloitte's US Wealth Management practice. https://manageria.biz/2016/06/17/will-the-30-trillion-great-wealth-transfer-change-the-way-of-financial-advising/

The following story is a case in point.

Cameron's mother died unexpectedly when Cameron was twenty-five years of age. It was the first time Cameron met his mother's financial and legal advisors. Still in shock from his mother's death, he felt very vulnerable and intimidated walking into the very modern legal offices on 8th Avenue in New York for the first time. He grasped very little of what he was being told.

To avoid being thought stupid, he avoided asking any questions, even when his mind could form one, and he left as soon as he could. When he shared this experience with his college friends, one of them advised Cameron to transfer his wealth to one of his brother's fellow college graduates, whom he said invested only in socially conscious corporations. This fit with Cameron's values, so he proceeded with the transfer. Within eight months, he had lost two-thirds of his inheritance due to the investor's lack of experience in investing.

In a survey of 1,000-plus investors that MFS Investment Management conducted in 2013, 75 percent of clients said their children had never even met their financial advisors. *InvestmentNews*, an industry publication, surveyed 544 advisors in 2015 and found that 66 percent of heirs take their inheritance and leave their deceased parents' advisors. "Lack of relationship" is the number one reason, cited by 30 percent of advisors surveyed.[8]

Discontinuity between generations and a lack of familiarity with the family financial advisors can pose a risk to the financial assets and to the family members' well-being. Millennials recognize that retirement saving should begin in early adulthood, but about 41 percent have not yet started, according to the 2016 Wells Fargo Millennial Study. The Wells Fargo study also revealed that millennials are open to coaching and education, and 71 percent of millennials would find value in having a financial coach to help

---

8. Joanne Cleaver, "Why Your Parents' Financial Advisor Asks About You," August 13, 2015, US News & World Report website, http://money.usnews.com/money/personal-finance/mutual-funds/articles/2015/08/13/why-your-parents-financial-advisor-asks-about-you

them understand retirement plans.[9] As promised in the introduction, chapter 3 focuses on the proprietary research conducted by The Williams Group that forms the basis of the 10-Question Quiz.[10] In that chapter, we explore more fully the implications of the primary drivers of successful wealth transfer. The research identifies the causes behind the 70 percent failure rate and highlights the differences between families who succeed in transitioning their wealth and those who fail.

Chapter 2 Summary

The high-net-worth family of today has become more complex and diverse, so the historic way of passing on wealth no longer suffices. A collectively agreed-on succession plan and well-prepared next generations are critical to a successful transfer of assets.

Millennials recognize that retirement saving should begin in early adulthood, but about 41 percent have not yet started.

The economic, social, and political background of wealth generators and designated recipients covers a wide range and influences their modus operandi. Millennials, the largest group of wealth recipients, recognize that retirement saving should begin in early adulthood, but about 41 percent have not yet started. The good news is that millennials are open to coaching and education, and most would find value in having a financial coach to help them understand retirement plans.

Affluent parents share similar and very legitimate con-

9. 2016 Wells Fargo Millennial Study, https://www08.wellsfargomedia.com/assets/pdf/commercial/retirement-employee-benefits/perspectives/2016-millennial-retirement-study.pdf.
10. The Williams Group, proprietary research performed between 1975 and 2001. Appendix I details the research for those who would like to further understand the investigative process.

cerns about the impact of wealth on their offspring. To ensure successful wealth transitions that preserve family unity and harmony, along with the financial assets, we can take what we have learned over fifty-two years of field studies with affluent families and implement proactive planning and preparing of families and heirs.

Discontinuity between generations and a lack of familiarity with the family's financial advisors can result in unprepared heirs changing financial advisors and estate planners. This can pose a risk to the financial assets and to the well-being of the family members.

CHAPTER

3

Main Drivers of Family Harmony—The Odds Are Not in Your Favor

"Problems cannot be solved by the
same level of thinking that created them."

—Albert Einstein

In all intergenerational wealth transfers, the question "How good is my plan?" arises.

This question means different things to different people. The lawyer hears one thing, the accountant another, and the children hear yet another.

Traditionally, financial advisors and estate planners have focused on three major areas:

1. Preservation (of assets)

2. Governance (or control of assets)

3. Taxation (issues that might diminish assets)

Financial advisors and estate planners are so well educated and trained in these three areas that the percentage of errors and oversights they make appears to get smaller with every passing year. In general, the research showed that professional advisors do a credible job of wealth preservation, governance, and taxation reduction. Less than 5 percent of failed wealth-transition plans are attributable to issues like faulty planning, poor tax advice, and inadequate document preparation. Often families paying for their advice develop a false sense of preparedness. While tax, legal, and financial planning is essential, this is an incomplete strategy for achieving success in estate transitions.

We have come to understand that there are two overarching aspects of wealth: financial assets and the family unity and harmony itself. History clearly indicates that both require equal attention, time, and money. Family unity and harmony are frequently ignored. This is often because successful wealth generators may be too busy and/or not know how to address relationship challenges within the family. Today family dynamics have changed, and financial complexity has increased. Given the evidence that around 70 percent of well-planned succession plans are derailed by family dynamics, we now know that it is critically important to prepare the family and the receivers for post-transition proactively.

Roy Williams, a pragmatist, asked this question: "What are the measurable differences between families who transitioned their wealth successfully and those who did not?" This struck at the heart of the problem, so The Williams Group polled many families who had transitioned their wealth. They interviewed more than 2,500 families and then examined data on 750 additional families. By the time the study[11] was completed, data had been collected on

---

11. Appendix 1 details the research for those who would like to understand the investigative process further.

3,250 transitioned families, and clear differences between successful and unsuccessful families stood out.

What Do Successful Wealth Transitions Require?

The two most critical elements of a successful wealth transition are as follows:

1. **Total family involvement and proactive preparation of the family**—Identification of family values, development of a family wealth mission/purpose statement, a glossary, alignment of these documents with the estate plans, identification of needs the family has and the roles to fulfill those needs, who will fill the roles, and development of qualifications and performance standards for those roles. Identification of individual aspirations and action plans for each member of the family.

2. **Acquisition of skill sets:**

   A. An integrative process based on openness and clear, authentic communication

   B. Trust—reliability, sincerity, competence, and caring

   C. Teamwork and consensus building

What Are the Critical "Checkpoints" to Use in Evaluating My Wealth-Transition Plan?

The research suggested two levels of examination. The first is condensed into a 10-Question Quiz to compare your wealth transition plan against the wealth-transition plans of those who have gone before you and succeeded. This quiz is typically completed by the family leader and is intended as a "quick read" on the family's readiness for transition. The weakness of the 10-Question Quiz is that it is only one individual's perception.

The second level of examination is a 50-Question Family Readiness Assessment to obtain the viewpoints of all the family members. We write more about this in chapter 4.

So that you can assess your wealth-transition plan, we have included the 10-Question Quiz here. After the quiz, we will examine each of these ten questions or principles in detail and review their relationship to a successful transition of wealth.

To how many of the following statements can you answer "Yes"?

"What are the measurable differences between families who transitioned their wealth successfully and those who did not?"

10-Question Quiz To Assess Your Wealth-Transition Plan	Yes or No
1. Does your family have a mission statement that spells out the overall purpose of your wealth?	
2. Does the entire family participate in most important decisions, such as defining a mission for your wealth?	
3. Do all family heirs have the option of participating in management of the family's assets?	
4. Do heirs understand their future roles, and have they "bought into" those roles and look forward to performing in them?	
5. Have the heirs reviewed the family's estate plans and documents?	
6. Do your current wills, trust, and other documents make most asset distributions based on family members' readiness rather than their age?	
7. Does your family mission include creating incentives and opportunities for heirs?	

8.	Are the younger children in your family encouraged to participate in your family's philanthropic grant-making decisions?	
9.	Does your family consider family unity to be just as important as family financial strength?	
10.	Does your family communicate well and meet regularly to discuss issues and changes?	
	Total number of "yes" answers	

A Closer Look at the 10-Question Quiz

Let's look at each of these questions in the quiz and what they assess, in detail.

Question 1: Does your family have a written mission statement that spells out the purpose of your wealth?

What does our family stand for? What are our values? How can we ensure that our family values are carried over from generation to generation?

The answers to these questions by the entire family are recorded on the family values chart. These values form the basis for the Family Wealth Mission Statement, a vital step in setting the course for the present and future direction. These values are the amalgamation of the entire family, including in-laws, grandchildren older than sixteen, and spouses. The process of identifying the family values and creating the family wealth mission/purpose statement is as much of a galvanizing process as the family wealth mission/purpose itself.

Once the mission/purpose is established, it is important to identify the actual behaviors that enable the family to live the mission on a daily basis.

A shared family wealth mission/purpose brings a sense of harmony to the family, provides a compass, and is something all family members can refer back to when making decisions. A family wealth mission/purpose provides family members with a sense of family that extends into future generations.

This is not a simple mission statement. It focuses on the question of the purpose of the wealth. For example, is the wealth intended to provide a level of comfort for the family members? Is it to provide educational and experiential opportunities? Is it for upcoming generations to build on and to fund their business or societal goals? Is it for philanthropic purposes? Or is it a balance among a number of goals?

A family wealth mission/purpose statement is not limited to parental goals. It is a declaration of the entire

What does our family stand for? What are our values? How can we ensure that our family values are carried over from generation to generation?

family that can transform the family forever, just as the Declaration of Independence changed the relationship of the United States to its country of origin and the future of the world. The power of making this kind of declaration is it sets an intentional course as opposed to allowing the drift of general interpretation be the guide.

The Family Wealth Mission Statement drives the family's professional advisors, rather than the other way around. A clearly written Family Wealth Mission Statement provides unifying guidance for professional advisors, avoids conflicts, resolves disputes and impasses, and provides forward-looking guidance as new circumstances and situations emerge. It greatly improves the efficiency and cost of the planning process. It enables professional advisors to respond promptly in advising courses of action as new legislation and rules emerge. It goes beyond the preservation, governance, and taxation issues to define the purpose of the wealth, not just its retention. It is the intersection of the settler's intentions and the shared meaning behind those intentions. As a trial lawyer once said to us, "having both of those documents in the same filing cabinet saves enormous cost."

A family wealth mission/purpose statement provides a map for the journey along with the long-term targets, goals, and destination. The shared family mission brings a sense of harmony to the family and models behaviors for younger family members, providing them with a sense of family that extends into future generations.

Declaring that the wealth is to "take care of my spouse and children" is what you want to accomplish. How it is accomplished, and what the family wants to do with the wealth in the broader context, is the purpose of the family wealth mission/purpose statement. It might have specific declarations that enable you to set priorities to accomplish the following:

- Create incentives for family member's participation and/or education.

- Create opportunity for personal and business growth.

- Empower the family.

- Encourage community involvement.

- Help our family grow as individuals, each fulfilling his or her own destiny.

- Offer every child an opportunity to take a role to address identified needs of the family and contribute in their own way.

- Share a portion of our gifts through our philanthropy and promote the values our family has developed.

The following objectives are realized through the process of developing a Family Wealth Mission Statement:

- Help family members set objectives for personal learning and growth.

- Have family members identify roles, qualifications required, and observable, measurable standards for performance of those roles that family members may claim, if they are qualified or desire to become qualified.

- Help the family develop knowledge and values through their philanthropic activities.

- Once you have developed a clear mission that is based on the established family values, then the strategies to attain that mission become easier to evaluate, measure, define, and change as time passes.

A family wealth mission/purpose statement provides a map for the journey along with the long-term targets, goals, and destination.

Appendix 2 contains several examples of family wealth mission/purpose statements. The following two examples from families illustrate carefully thought out, heavily debated, and family-wide adopted written mission statements.

"To maximize the equitable transfer of my assets in a way that will enable and encourage my family to work for the benefit of humanity."

"Through God's grace; dream, plan, and grow closer to God and each other using the resources entrusted to our care for the benefit of God's work, family, business, people, and community."

Question 2: Does the entire family participate in most important decisions, such as the definition of the mission for the family wealth?

Successful families involve the entire family in articulating, sharing, and developing a family values chart and a Family Wealth Mission Statement. Together they are making important decisions that will affect them in the future.

Prior to the wealth transition, all age-appropriate family members are included in family get-togethers and family meetings.

Include bloodline family members, spouses, blended and adopted family members, grandparents, and significant others/fiancées.

The key phrases here are "entire family" and "important decisions." Having the *entire family* participate, including children age sixteen and above, begins to set expectations, as well as boundaries. It begins to define, for children, what is expected of them as participants in the discussion about *important decisions.* It also begins to define the importance of becoming competent on issues on which they personally wish to comment.

Requesting the entire family's participation creates an inclusive, considerate, and welcoming environment for all family members. This environment, the conversational exchange and lifetime learning, time together, and the growing connection as a family in turn tends to modify and shape some individual extreme viewpoints. People who have lived long lives often become more understanding of the human condition, more understanding of those who have not faced crisis, and patient with the passions of youth.

We initially believed that the earlier this process of participation is implemented, the more likely the wealth transition would be successful. However, we have found, over the years, that with commitment, change can occur at any age. The first time we encountered a late age change was when we advised a ninety-year-old grandfather. He realized that his grandsons were directionless and floundering, and trying to force his work ethic on them was not working, so he sought coaching. He involved the entire family in the process. He said he learned so much about each of his family members, especially his grandchildren, and most valuable of all was the connection he was able to make with all his family members before it was too late.

Having the entire family participate, including children age sixteen and above, begins to set expectations, as well as boundaries.

During this process, it is important for family leaders to set standards for courtesy, consideration, listening, embracing diversity, and welcoming new family members. There is value in receiving a wide range of input and ideas, but do not lose sight of the fact that the family is gathered together to make decisions.

Role modeling by the parents through participative leadership, honest listening, and consideration is a very important part of this process. If leadership is absent from the family meeting, it sends a message that says, "My time and personal mission are more important than any of you." Modeling occurs, for better or for worse.

Our research shows that involvement of the entire family in the decision-making process during the parents' lifetime is one of the key differences between successful and unsuccessful families. More often than not, including the entire family results in the upcoming generation being committed to carrying on the estate in accordance with the family values.

Although this process is more challenging and time-consuming to begin with, in the long run it saves time, money, and unnecessary conflict. When Mom and/or Dad avoids the trap of attempting to dictate "the future" to their children from beyond the grave, they also avoid causing a split in the unity of the family and missing the opportunity for generational unity.

However, just because parents accept the family's input, it does not mean that they hand over authority or control. It does mean, based on timing and maturity, that they will share information with the family, allow family members to provide their input and to influence major transition decisions, and receive their input with respect and consideration.

If leadership is absent from the family meeting, it sends a message that says, "My time and personal mission are more important than any of you."

Although the leaders of a family who own/control the family business or wealth during their lifetime hold great authority, it is unrealistic to believe that this authority can be reliably projected into the future based on documents developed privately with legal counsel. There is a growing body of instances in which parents make unilateral decisions regarding family members and the transitioning of the estate that turn out to be neither effective nor unifying for the family.

Most importantly, our research shows quite clearly that if the family wealth mission/purpose statement, objectives, and important decisions are defined and dictated only by the founders/leaders of the family, almost inevitably, profound divergence will occur once the family members assume (or are assigned) responsibility. This is because they were excluded from the conversations prior to the transfer of wealth. Too often, this results in family members (or their spouses) resorting to litigation, rejection, nonparticipation, family separation, passive–aggressive behavior, and any other tactic they can use to get their viewpoints considered. This could have been done much more effectively in a conversational mode with coaching support when the family values were identified and the family wealth mission/purpose statement was first developed. In these situations, sometimes the only unifying factor appears to be the siblings sharing legal expenses as they attempt to have the will overturned or the trust agreement broken.

Question 3. Do all family heirs have the option of participating in management of the family assets?

Of course, the critical word here is "option." Successful wealth transitions include early inclusion of the thinking and wishes of family members and spouses. Historically, the notion that the heir will be responsible for assets once his or her parents are gone was a consistent estate-planning pattern. What is more successful is to reach out to family members, early on, and begin to prepare them to accomplish the following:

- Be concerned about the quality of management of the family assets. Understand the roles of the advisory team, be able to assess their competence, and if necessary, be involved in the selection of new ones.

- Acquire a basic education on the fundamental drivers of success and failure of the family business. Gain a general understanding of the long-term vision.

- Participate in a fundamental financial education program using a portion of the family assets as the platform from which to learn and gain understanding of financial reports, trusts, and estate planning. Learn how to make decisions as a team about the family assets, business, and philanthropy.

- Know that family members can have a role in the management of those assets based on their qualifications, level of competence, and interest.

In our research, one aspect that is critical to the process of successful families is matching family members' interests and competencies with the roles that are available. Certainly, one would not urge a family member who is a competent portrait painter to be saddled with the daily management of interest-bearing investment accounts or the performance of hedge fund managers, for example.

All family members attended the first meeting of the Davi family and their coach. One thirty-year-old family member, a son, arrived two hours late and looking disheveled. He had not held a steady job since college. Before he arrived, one of the family members openly referred to him as "a loser." During eighteen months of periodic family meetings held to build trust and communication while developing the family values and the family wealth mission/purpose statement, it became apparent that the family held him in disdain because he had no interest in business.

Because of their competitive family culture, the thinking was, "If you are not, or do not ascribe to be, a business person, CEO, or president, you are a nobody."

However, when the discussion and planning was about philanthropy, the son saw possibilities to work in a different kind of environment. His energy and enthusiasm for the potential within the family foundation were contagious. He plunged into the role, working feverishly to learn more and become competent to make "good" philanthropic decisions. He blossomed.

Two years later, after a series of family meetings, further education, and experience, the now well-groomed heir was made "lead goose" (a term used to describe the person who takes on the leader role in a team - similar to a lead goose in a flock of geese) of the family foundation. The transformation was a joy to him and the family, and after another two years, he was made president of the foundation. He had found his life's purpose, and as a result, his confidence and self-esteem increased.

Rather than cause family members to feel separated, unaccountable, or unimportant in relationship to family assets (which they may depend on), it is important to assure each family member that there is a role they can play, if they desire. It is a matter of defining that role and preparing them for it. The portrait painter might play a role in overseeing the family philanthropy devoted to supporting the arts. In that role, he or she could evaluate the impact of, and better uses for, the family's philanthropy dollars and discuss new opportunities. The family's needs generate these roles. Other roles may be ensuring communication of family business updates, creating a website for family communication, or even organizing the family business meeting locations and logistics.

Family members can discover options to participate by deliberately including all family members instead of rigidly and automatically excluding those who do not appear to fit in, or perhaps worse, providing them a title or a position to give a false sense of contribution.

Question 4. Do heirs understand their future roles, and have they "bought into" those roles and look forward to performing in them?

Once the family wealth mission is created, the *strategy and structure* for attaining this mission are developed.

The family identifies which needs exist. Then they will decide which roles will fulfill these needs, which family members are best suited for each role, and who wants to take on a particular role. Together with the role-development team, the family decides on the qualifications, competency, and performance standards for each role.

In short, there needs to be an overarching, proven process that is sustainable and will keep everyone on target, translating their individual wishes into a consensus that leads to specific estate instructions and actions. When consensus exists within the family, the clarity it provides can dramatically accelerate resolution of the complex decisions advisory professionals wrestle with. Because of the focus and clarity that is brought to the process within the family, the cost of outside assistance is reduced.

Once the family wealth mission is created, the strategy and structure for attaining this mission are developed.

A vital aspect we saw represented in the research is the importance of self-generated roles. We see a direct correlation among the roles generated by the family's needs, the family members' sense of belonging, and buy-in to the family legacy.

It is equally important that family members of successfully transitioned estates are not forced into a responsibility. Our research shows that when sudden deaths or departures occur, successful families often bring in temporary managers (family and/or nonfamily). Those temporary managers come with the clear understanding that this is a special situation, that their tenure is expected to be temporary, and that an active search will get under way to determine the best replacement. The temporary manager often transitions into a full-time mentor to the family member who eventually replaces them.

The careful assessment of family member's interests, and the proper match-up with the family's needs, qualifications, and performance standards, is important to the family members' long-term satisfaction and performance in the job. In addition, when family members "buy in" to their roles, the necessary preparations and active participation in developing their own qualifications and competencies seem to follow.

Successful families agree that early awareness and preparation of family members for clearly defined future roles brings a great deal of stability into the family. This contrasts with the turmoil of family members "jockeying around" for roles as their interests change, new spouses enter the family, roles change, and strategies are adjusted. Key to resolving these issues is the family team's development of qualification and performance standards.

Family members' interests will change. They mature, refine, and redefine their individual objectives at several points in their lives. We have found that the successful families keep the communication channels open by meeting with family members frequently. Those meetings privately check the next generations' "temperature" to see if they are still interested and are making expected progress in developing the necessary competencies. If the family leader detects a waning of interest or a failure to keep up with the requisite competency development, then it is time to reassess the role and direction for the next generations and to discuss that openly and directly with them. Such a discussion proves to be a relief, not a burden. They are usually first to realize that they are falling behind the progress curve he or she agreed on, and in some cases, that the role initially chosen was not a match.

Question 5. Have the heirs reviewed the family estate plans and documents?

This question addresses communication, openness, and instilling a sense of responsibility in the family members. Reading the words and seeing the numbers in the documents has a surprising impact on family members and benefactors. As Samuel Johnson once wrote, "Depend on it, sir, when a man knows he is to be hanged in a fortnight, it concentrates his mind wonderfully." Not that a hanging is in store, but the risk of an estate landing on uninformed and unprepared family members can result in chaos.

The reality of planned responsibility (as a steward for some portion of the family wealth) hits home when people see it in black and white.

We have also seen family members who, after viewing the will and relevant preconditions, revealed to their parents that they had medical reasons that precluded them from having children. This avoided inclusion of a futile historical family standard—"childbearing condition"—in their inheritance entitlement. Again, it goes back to the policies of inclusion and openness for the family.

Successful families agree that early awareness and preparation of family members for clearly defined future roles brings a great deal of stability into the family.

The conversation about adoption is often one that is opened for the first time for the entire family to explore when they develop the definition of "family" for the family wealth mission/purpose statement. Stepchildren, adopted children, bloodlines, and spouses all become part of the family discussion on defining who is a beneficiary and family member.

Children who do not know the extent of the family's wealth are unable to discuss what they might be inclined to do with it when it is inherited. Obviously, adults who read conditions that they think are onerous or intrusive can discuss this with their parents only while everyone is still alive. Often these discussions and open dialogues prove to be among the most treasured moments family members recall later.

Another finding from our research is that parental fears of wealth creating a "disincentive" disappear in most cases as the next generations experience growth and personal development and experience their parents' recognition, appreciation, and acknowledgment of their achievements. This often generates a mutual recognition of the parents by the family members.

Finally, as communication and trust increase, even sensitive issues can be discussed openly with the help of a coach. This takes a great deal of finesse and skill so that no one is offended or embarrassed. Issues such as being gay, unfair distribution of assets, perceived grievances, or even the inability to conceive a child can lead to challenging conversations.

In the coaching process, family meetings on developing the family wealth mission/purpose statement, structure, strategy, and role selection tend to uncover previously hidden concerns held by family members and the parents. The important conclusion here is that parents who involve the family in the documents and provide them to the family for review and comment are uniformly more successful in family wealth transitions than those parents who keep the contents of the documents to themselves.

Question 6. Do your current wills, trusts, and other documents make most asset distributions based on family members' readiness rather than their age?

Tradition and certainty die hard. Because it is easy to measure age numerically and with specific dates, precise asset distributions are often based on simplistic, chronological standards of age. However, our research indicates that parents' levels of understanding of their offspring vary widely in terms of factors such as maturity, preparedness, and readiness to make use of the assets. One family member said, "We saw the precision of age as the lawyer's refuge." Another said, "I can give my daughter and son the same amount of money. He will come back and ask for more; she will come back with more."

Simple rules such as "one-third on the twenty-first birthday, one-third on the thirty-first birthday, and the final third on the forty-first birthday" are easy to state in documents and easy to execute.

In the event of unforeseen changes required for health reasons, marriage, divorce, disability, or any of a number of other circumstances, estate planners often build in the ability to vary some conditions. It is not possible to construct a document that applies to all possible eventualities. Flexibility tends to broaden the language, which increases the trustee's legal liability in the event of a "wrong" decision. Therefore, most distributions fall back on precise ages and dates for entitlements.

In contrast, the most successful estates transition wealth based on a series of events or accomplishments. For example, a stipulation might be that the first distribution is available at age thirty-five if the beneficiary has been fully employed for the preceding five years and has received increases in responsibility with pay commensurate to reflect that responsibility. These are observable and measurable standards.

"I can give my daughter and son the same amount of money. He will come back and ask for more; she will come back with more."

If the beneficiaries fail to meet these standards, they receive an "extension" for another five-year period. Some families and professional advisors are opposed to "standards," but when the entire family develops the standards and agrees to live by them, they work well. Age alone is a poor qualifier.

As Ponch Soreson entered his late eighties, he began to rethink his years of hesitation about turning the business over to his only daughter, Karen. She knew the business, having worked there all her adult life. He was slowing down, tired more easily, and couldn't put in the twelve-hour days of only a few years earlier.

Ponch had held tightly to the reins of leadership and kept Karen from becoming the company president of the family corporation. With his advancing age, he knew she'd have to take the reins.

Ponch called Karen into the office and made the announcement that he was finally promoting her to president. She was ready, and so was he. He was shocked when his daughter said, "Daddy, I'm turning sixty-five next week and scheduled for retirement. Maybe one of the grandkids might be interested, but now one's a doctor, and the other is a musician. I doubt either of them is interested in giving up their professional careers."

Question 7. Does your family mission include creating incentives and opportunities for heirs?

Successful family wealth transitions include incentives and opportunities to build a sense of "fun" and "involvement" for the family. Rather than entering a dependency relationship, or a form of family welfare by giving each family member the tax-free $14,000 gift allowed by the IRS annually, leaders in one family went out of their way to develop ways for the family members to earn that same amount each year.

With the help of a coach, the family interviewed money managers to work with family members. The chosen money manager and the family members managed these funds based on the "Investment Policy Statement" the family developed with their coach. The family members invested the money, monitored the process monthly, and reported on the results quarterly. At the end of the year, it was agreed that the family leaders and the managing family members would split the profits. It surprised everyone how often the profit split was about equal to the annual gift exclusion allowed under the IRS code. Instead of being passive recipients of unearned income, the family members and parents built competence, confidence, and self-esteem.

In another case, a young heir was given responsibility for several decisions regarding the family foundation. If she set standards for performance (to accompany each grant given by the family foundation) and selected charities that attained those standards, then she was given more funds to allocate the next year. Frequently, the family leaders gave each of the family members steadily increasing responsibility for a specific amount of the family's wealth.

The next generation may want to pursue impact investing, a growing trend among millennials to invest in companies, organizations, and funds that have a beneficial impact on social or environmental concerns and produce financial gains. The investment policy statement would include impact investing as an avenue for the family to pursue as a team, and as part of their mission. Creating incentives and opportunities for family members is an important part of how a mission statement becomes real. It is also an important part of how family members learn to engage and include their advisor(s).

These simple incentives link performance to reward, keep communication channels active and open, and build self-esteem in the family members. Incentives build a sense of continued learning and an appreciation that the rewards go to those who "mind the store."

Question 8. Are younger children encouraged to participate in the family's philanthropic grant-making decisions?

Although it is impossible to apply across-the-board generalizations, many who work closely with high earners observe that a growing number reject parenting styles of past generations. Instead, they want close, warm relationships with their children. Also, they are concerned about the effect of wealth on their children, and they use philanthropy to counter those effects.

Successful wealth-transition families encourage children to participate in the family's philanthropy decisions. This contributes to the overall good, provides a forum for exploring family values, and has the potential to contribute to the development of character.

Toby Neugebauer, cofounder of Texas-based Quantum Energy Partners, and his wife took their nine- and eleven-year-old sons on a tour of some of the poorest places in the world. They visited the slums of Mumbai, the dirt-path villages in Africa, and orphanages of China. The parents' intention was to expand their children's understanding of those less privileged and to visit some of the organizations funded by the family foundation, which is called "Matthew 6:20."

In one successful wealth-transition family, the children, beginning at ages ten to twelve, were encouraged to talk about what they thought was important. In translating their concerns (values) via the family foundation, the parents taught them the importance of family values and the importance of accountability (following their family's contributions to see if the money did what it was supposed to do).

The family members gradually learned to ask questions, expect accountability, and value feedback and reporting. They began to shift their charitable interests by concentrating their contributions to the most responsive and effective charities. A charity's ratio of direct to indirect expenses and the portion of its funds that went to fund-raising and to the charity's purpose became important issues. These issues, in turn, fostered increased family discussion and a steadily increasing sense of the family's values as young family members came to know more about the family's charitable work. Over time, family members came to depend on the younger family members for major philanthropic decisions.

Incentives build a sense of continued learning and an appreciation that the rewards go to those who "mind the store."

Philanthropy proved to be a fertile training ground for the children with respect to family values. It also substantially accelerated their skills at translating family values into individual action and decision making.

Question 9. Does your family consider family unity to be just as important as family financial strength?

This issue is known as the "balance point" for successful families. Focusing solely on passing the maximum amount of wealth to the children deprives families of the time and experiences needed to build relationships and to reach agreement on the mission for the family wealth. Failure to involve the entire family in identifying the family values, creating a family wealth mission/purpose statement, and making future decisions on strategy and roles diminishes the sense of family unity.

Successful families focus first on family unity and second on maximizing the value of the assets to be transferred. When the focus is reversed, it is common for family leaders to believe that any money spent for professional teaching and coaching of the family is "an unnecessary expense." Consequently, they choose not to invest resources to prepare their family proactively.

When family members are insufficiently prepared for succession, often once the wealth transition occurs, longstanding disagreements and resentments concerning competence and control quickly surface among siblings, spouses, and cousins.

Successful families uniformly focus pre-transition on building family relationships, identifying family values, developing the family wealth mission/purpose statement, building authentic trust, ensuring ongoing open communication, and preparing family members proactively as the essential foundation for growth, unity, and family harmony. They recognize that with this foundation, the accumulation and wise use of family assets and the broader mission of their philanthropic goals will naturally follow and serve to reinforce spiri-

Successful families focus first on family unity and second on maximizing the value of the assets to be transferred.

tuality[12] within the family through the generations. The ability to articulate these priorities to family members, both in family meetings and individually, leaves no sense of ambiguity about what Mom and Dad want for the family. It teaches the family to get over

---

12. In this book, *spirituality* means values such as unconditional love, seeking first to understand and then to be understood, and the feeling that there is a higher calling to life, demonstrating a long-term purpose for existence. Doing good because good is good to do.

the dispute, work for a mutual resolution, and get on with their lives as a family team. Parents who simply "give the order" to "get along" are unsuccessful.

Families almost always lack the skills to make this happen in isolation. Successful transitioning families inevitably bring in outside professional coaching, just as they historically have brought in lawyers, accountants, and estate planners (and driver's education for their teenagers). "Family comes first" is the motto of families who are successful in transitioning their wealth.

Question 10. Does your family communicate well and meet regularly as a family to discuss issues and changes?

According to our research, the leaders of families who have successful transitions seem to share certain rules of communications within the family. For one family in particular, no business meeting was so important that it could not be interrupted for a phone call from a family member (who, in turn, was encouraged to refrain from calling during business hours unless it was essential).

The family routinely met for seasonal get-togethers on holidays and prioritized family time. The entire family also scheduled at least one family meeting annually to discuss business issues (separate from holiday get-togethers.) The topics most frequently discussed in these meetings dealt with forward planning and informing the family of newly shared responsibilities and business/asset developments.

Communication involved the entire family, including spouses. It was open, and everyone was sought out for thoughts, opinions, and recommendations. The family meetings usually lasted for one or two days. Absolute confidentiality was maintained within the family, and family leaders made strong efforts to make certain that everyone was heard.

Families that fail transitions frequently hold family meetings, but their meetings are often unsuccessful due to a lack of skilled coaching or facilitation. The family leaders develop agendas that focused on their own issues and priorities, and they dominated and controlled the meeting. The family members experienced these meetings as "lecture time" versus "participation time." Some thought that the parents were attempting to program or control them. As a result, the family members considered these meetings a waste of time and money.

Some unsuccessful wealth-transition families combine family meetings with holiday events and try to control the meetings. This often leads to high levels of stress and anxiety for the entire family throughout the holiday.

How to Score Your Answers

Historical data from the 2,500 families we worked with enabled us to confirm the importance of the ten checklist items by comparing the answers of successful transition families with those who were unsuccessful. In general, they divide into three areas of comparability:

- Families who answer "yes" to seven or more of the ten questions in the quiz are closely correlated with those families who have successfully transitioned their wealth. They are most likely the one family in three who will transition their values and their wealth into a relatively harmonious environment for the benefit of their children and grandchildren, while preserving a family unified in its belief that the individuals in the family are just as important as the wealth in the family.

- Families who answer "yes" to four to six of the ten questions are likely to benefit substantially from efforts to improve the levels of trust and communication within their family. This is fundamental to preparing their family members for wealth and responsibility. In the absence of a substantial effort, however, this group will remain most closely correlated with the 70 percent of the families who do not effectively transition their wealth. This is the "high return" group that can achieve the largest improvement in their odds of transition success with the least amount of work.

- Families who answer "yes" to three or fewer of the ten questions are closely correlated to those families who fail to transition their wealth and values successfully. Those families are characterized by a dissipation of wealth among the family members, infighting and hostility within the family, and a loss of family unity in the next generations. It is important to note that those situations can be changed for the better. It requires family leadership and professional coaching assistance to make the changes necessary to increase the odds of a successful transition.

The questions in this quiz are useful for annual checks to determine how the family is doing.

Chapter 3 Summary

Chapter 3 provides the 10-Question Quiz, along with explanations, for heads of families to use in assessing the family's readiness for future wealth transfer.

The Williams Group's definition of wealth includes the family itself. A successful wealth transfer results in the financial assets being transferred as planned, the family being responsible and accountable, and family unity and harmony being retained across generations. Attaining family unity and harmony prior to the transition is critical.

The 10-Question Quiz is a useful tool that families can use to assess the viability of existing intergenerational wealth transfer plans. This chapter explains why each question is important and describes measurable differences between families who successfully transitioned their wealth and those who did not.

Given the evidence that around 70 percent of well-planned succession plans are derailed by family dynamics, we know that it is vital to take the necessary proactive steps to prepare the family and heirs for the transition of wealth.

4

The First Step: Taking the Initiative to Beat the Odds (Here's Your Road Map)

"There are risks and costs to a program of action. But they are far less than the long-range risks and costs of comfortable inaction."

—John Fitzgerald Kennedy

You might expect that with all the books purchased on self-help, how to succeed, succession planning, and trust and communication, this world would be filled with many more successful, happy people and more successful estate transitions. But unfortunately, many transitions fail. The breakdown of trust and communication continues to be the dominant reason for failed succession and wealth transitions.

Given the often-recited aphorisms like "Knowledge is power" and "Know the truth and the truth shall set you free," people question how knowledge of the causes of failure can be translated into freedom from failure.

Knowing What's Wrong vs. Doing What's Right

After interviewing many families, we arrived at the conclusion that most families understand what should be done, and what could be done, but lacked the will or the skills to put that knowledge into practice. It is much like understanding the precise mechanics of making a basketball shot, while knowing (as a nonprofessional recreational player) that from twenty-five feet out, it is mostly a matter of luck if you get the ball into the basket.

Football coaches, the US military, and other institutions that are dependent on teaching effective team performance understand this gap between knowledge and proficiency. US military field-grade officers attend the Command School at Fort Leavenworth, Kansas, as a critical part of their military career development. There they study past battles and mistakes made by other military commanders throughout history. Then they move to the "sandbox," where they study the battles in three dimensions. Then it's out to the field for practice maneuvers. Finally, they develop and practice interservice and intercountry maneuvers to perfect their skills of execution. Often there are casualties (and even deaths) as they test their ability and hone their skills to perform in the field.

The difference between knowing and doing is large, and it is the determining factor between failure and success. That difference can be bridged only by practice. Practice is most effective when conducted in an environment as close to real-world situations as possible. Practice needs to be measured, evaluated, refined, and performed repeatedly.

When we look at individuals who are particularly skilled in sports, we see them practice much more than the average athlete. For example, Michael Jordan shoots one thousand baskets after every practice. Ben Hogan used to hit one thousand golf balls every day.

The same is true of a football coach who works from the "X"s and "O"s of the blackboard to the drills on the field to the intrasquad practice prior to the actual game. It is only then that the team understands the relationships, timing, competencies, and shortcomings of the players and can thus execute plays successfully.

The difference between knowing and doing is large, and it is the determining factor between failure and success. That difference can be bridged through practice.

The legendary Green Bay Packers of the Coach Vince Lombardi era practiced so strenuously that the players privately considered Sunday's game day as a "relief day." They were as prepared as their practice could make them. Winning, as a result of perfectly and intensively executed plays, was natural for that team. Vince Lombardi made his football team practice the same plays over and over for hours. He told his team, "Fatigue makes cowards of us all, so when you're tired, toward the end of a game, you will always revert back to your old patterns of play, and the only way to avoid this is to practice, practice, practice." The team relied on expertly honed skills developed through recurrent practice as a tool for winning.

The same can be true of family members, whose tools for winning include trust and communication to address conflicts, especially in the heat of the moment. Some strategies may be very destructive long term, such as the need for control. That is a fear-based need, and we parents, when we feel fear for our children, tend to use control as a tool to protect them.

The skills needed to develop communication and trust require time and use in challenging situations. When we work with families, they learn these skills by applying them to current, meaningful topics, which enables them to more easily navigate challenging conversations. The more they practice, the more they succeed (and the more important conversations can get addressed). Without this practice, they find themselves challenged when conflicts arise, and they revert to their old patterns. Just as Coach Lombardi suggested, the only way to avoid this is "...practice, practice, practice," so new skills become the new habit. Learning begins with declaring yourself a beginner. We will talk more about that a little later in this chapter.

Over the years, we have concluded that communication among family members cannot simply be theory. Family members must practice newly learned communication skills, especially during the most challenging of family interactions. This requires understanding, commitment, and discipline from the family leadership.

It is not simply a matter of the leaders of the family declaring, "From now on, we're all going to communicate!" That type of pressure, without training in the skills and without well-coached practice, will simply sow the seeds of deception, false compliance, and mistrust among family members. The family leader has to model the new skills and set the tone for learning for the rest of the family.

How this disciplined practice takes place in The Williams Group Process begins with the 10-Question Quiz that we covered in chapter 3. The score you attained on that quiz is the first indication of your family's trust and communication level. If the score that an individual attains on the 10 Question Quiz raises concerns, the next step is to have the entire family take the anonymous 50-Question Family Readiness Assessment. The answers to the fifty more detailed questions, based on a 1–5 scale, allows all family members to respond easily and honestly without fear of identification.

While the 10-Question Quiz about wealth transition has high reliability in its correlation with successful families and unsuccessful families, the reliability level is further improved, and the problem areas clearly pinpointed, if the entire family (including spouses and adult children) is given the opportunity to separately answer the fifty questions. We analyze, correlate, and culminate all responses in a written report and provide it to the family in person for open discussion.

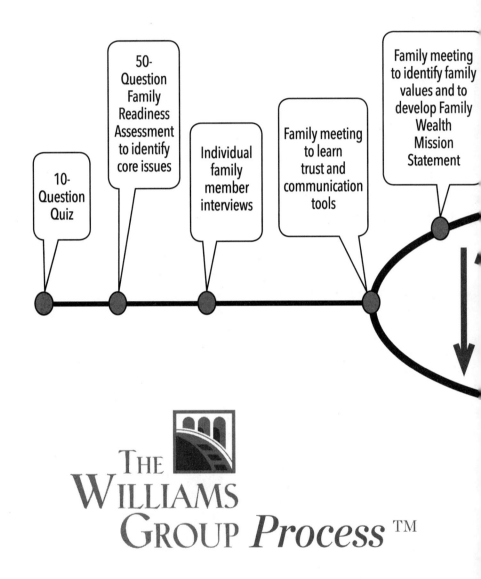

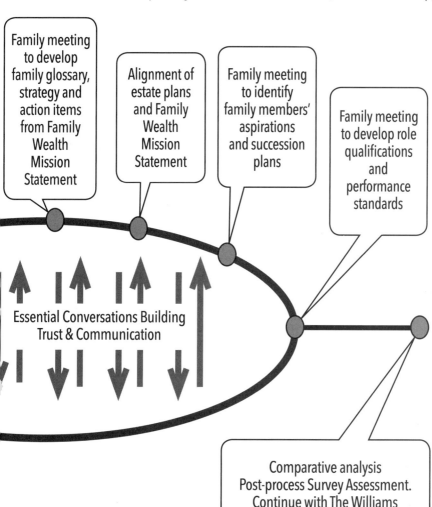

Family meeting to develop family glossary, strategy and action items from Family Wealth Mission Statement

Alignment of estate plans and Family Wealth Mission Statement

Family meeting to identify family members' aspirations and succession plans

Family meeting to develop role qualifications and performance standards

Essential Conversations Building Trust & Communication

Comparative analysis Post-process Survey Assessment. Continue with The Williams Advisory Group for next generation educational services

Over the course of many years, based on best practices, we have developed the tried and tested The Williams Group Process™. It provides a structure that allows the family to co-design their cornerstone on which all other aspects of the estate plan stand. It offers families a ten stage process over a period of eighteen months, on average, to prepare proactively for a successful succession and wealth transfer. The time frame is largely determined by the family's schedule.

Let's look at the ten steps in the process in detail.

1. Take the 10-Question Quiz to evaluate your wealth-transition plan.

If the score attained raises concerns, the next step is to consider the entire family in more detail. The ten wealth-transition questions are highly reliable in terms of their correlation with successful families and unsuccessful families. The ten-question reliability level is further improved and problem areas pinpointed if the entire family (including spouses and adult children) is given the opportunity to answer a more detailed set of questions separately and their responses are analyzed.

2. Take the 50-Question Quiz to get input from your entire family without fear or guilt.

After answering the 10-Question Quiz, your family may decide to complete the 50-Question Family Readiness Assessment. It is confidential, with no identifiers of individuals, and we will compile the results in a written report that we send to all family members. This report identifies the three core issues related to the key drivers of family unity and harmony during wealth transition.

Before we can begin to work with a family, it is imperative that we focus on the core issues. Otherwise, everyone spends time and resources taking care of symptoms. Next, we review this report with all family members and a Williams Group coach. If your family decides to use The Williams Group Process to address the threats to a successful succession and wealth transfer proactively, the family leader will sign the Evergreen Agreement. This document clarifies the terms of the engagement.

3. Interview each family member.

Family-member interviews are confidential, and the results are available to the coaches for the purpose of understanding the family. One of the things we've discovered along the journey to help families is the fact that someone needs to listen to the family members. Often, family life centers around managing the family's wealth or business(es) and evolves to reflect the priorities of the family leaders. It is typical that family life begins to be unbalanced around the business of managing assets. When the next generation is given an opportunity to be heard, they are often reinspired. In preparation for the fourth step, you will schedule your first family meeting.

4. Hold the first family meeting.

This first meeting sets the standard for all other family meetings. It is here where the family members begin the process of building trust and learning how important conversations will be held in ways that maintain people's dignity, protect their identities, and provide a forum for their voice to be heard. The purpose of the family coming together is to discuss family, family wealth, its impact, and opportunities. At the first meeting, the family members establish how they will work together to keep the meetings productive and safe. They identify important topics to discuss and engage in meaningful conversations that are important to strengthening trust and building clarity. The tools for improving communication, building trust, managing moods, and enhancing coordination are introduced in relevant moments. These conversations provide the landscape for future meetings.

5. Hold a family meeting to co-design family values and co-develop a Family Wealth Mission Statement and glossary.

In this meeting, we create graphic illustrations of the values and family wealth mission generated by the family itself. Often families frame these. This is typically a galvanizing process for the family that reestablishes connections, acceptance, and pride in belonging to the same family.

6. Hold a family meeting to develop a glossary for each word in the mission statement.

The purpose of the glossary is to ensure that everyone, including advisors, is in alignment with the same understanding and action items. It is an important part of the process for establishing a strategy, standards, and protocol. It is how the Family Wealth Mission Statement is incorporated into everyday practices. For example, if the word "education" appears in the mission statement, everyone agrees on what the standards are for education, such as obtaining a degree from an accredited institution. The financial advisor or even the legal advisor may then get involved in supporting the family to ensure that education is addressed in the financial plan and/or the trust documents.

7. Hold a family meeting to compare the estate-planning documents with the family's values and wealth mission.

To ensure that they are coordinated, we will identify the family's needs and roles that are needed to fulfill the family wealth mission and estate plans. We also will agree on the implementation strategy and share it with your family's professional advisors and estate-planning architects.

8. Hold a family meeting to explore family members' individual aspirations and succession plans.

Individual family members' goals and interests are then aligned with the various roles that emerged from the family wealth mission and estate plans. This is particularly important for family leaders as they begin to consider the next stage of their career during the succession planning process.

9. Hold a family meeting to develop qualification and performance standards for each role.

We develop these standards with the family. You can use them to fill the roles needed within the family and to hire external advisors.

10. Hold a family meeting to have the family complete the 50-Question Family Readiness Assessment a second time.

The purpose of taking the assessment a second time is to see how much the family has learned during the family meetings and The Williams Group Process, after taking the 50-Question Assessment the first time. We provide a pre- and post-comparative analysis that measures the family's growth in a written report to the family and review it with the family members and their coach. If the family or individual family members desire further coaching on role development, they can continue with The Williams Advisory Group (more information on this is included in chapter 8), who provide these services:

- Family coaching and mentoring

- Financial education support

- Family business consulting

- Family enterprise strategies and resources

- Support to the next generation to make investment or philanthropic decisions as a team

The 50-Question Family Readiness Assessment

The purpose of the 50-Question Family Readiness Assessment is to identify the three core issues related to the fundamental key drivers of family unity and harmony during wealth transition. It also provides a pre- and post-measuring tool of the growth of the family as a whole, with respect to trust and communication, heir preparedness, and alignment of mission and values.

It is important that the entire family, including spouses and children above the age of sixteen, is given the opportunity to participate in the survey. The individual responses to these questionnaires are kept anonymous, even among family members. This helps us avoid challenges to any individual's answers and helps ensure the highest degree of candid responses possible.

The analysis measures the following:

- **Trust and communication levels ("T&C")**—Specific areas of variance within the family with respect to the family's sense of the level of trust and communication they share.

- **Heir preparedness ("Heirs")**—The level of heirs' preparation for accountability and responsibility.

- **Mission/purpose clarity for family wealth ("Mission")**—The status of an agreed-upon family wealth mission built on family values.

Another reason to seek responses from the entire family is to reconcile differences in three core drivers. Often, in families that have shared ownership of the family business, there can be wide disparities across generations related to these core drivers.

Most frequently, tensions exist between the family members from the operating side of the family (e.g., the daughter of the founder who is running the family business or managing the assets) and the family members of the nonoperating side (e.g., the other daughter of the founder who is not running the business or managing the assets and is a passive recipient of income). Additionally, blended families often experience tensions among various family members.

The fifty-question family readiness assessment, combined with individual interviews, can reveal where areas of tension reside, where communication is breaking down, and who in the family feels included or excluded. These are critical pieces of knowledge that must be addressed if the upcoming generation is to experience a successful transition of the family wealth. Without addressing these problems, "shirtsleeves-to-shirtsleeves in three generations" is a high probability.

Although the fifty detailed questions are not included in this book, an example of a family's "pre- and post-coaching" bar graph is shown below. We use a fictitious name, "Eagle," to represent the family. We have permission to use this example, and we have changed identifying details to protect our actual client's confidentiality. The seven family members who responded are labeled A through G across the bottom of the graph. The graph represents responses of the parents, children, and their spouses. The questionnaires provide no indication as to which members of the family completed them.

"Eagle" Family Pre-Coaching Graphs— 50-Question Survey Results

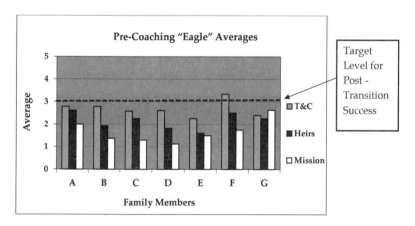

"Perfect" would be a score of 5 with a minimum goal of 3.0 for all family members in each category. From the graph above, it is evident that the Eagle family was operating with a generally low level of Trust and Communication (left, light gray) because the family member with the highest score (F) scored a little higher than 3.0, and the lowest member (E) scored less than 2.5.

The family perceived Heir Readiness (middle, dark gray) even lower on the scale, with a high of around 2.5 and a low of 1.5.

The Mission for the Family Wealth (white, far right) ranged uniformly low, between 1 and 2.5. In short, everyone in the family thought the family was unprepared for the transition and rated their need for assistance as relatively urgent. This indicates that, for the transition, there was likely to be disputes that could result in a breakdown in family unity, as well as potential litigation.

It is key to measure or quantify these core issues so they can be addressed.

At that point in time, family members' lack of trust was preventing everyone from declaring their "beginner" status (discussed below), thus preventing learning, preparation, and improvement in the family's odds of a successful transition.

These findings, combined with subsequent individual interviews, clearly pointed out the need for, and the direction of, remedial actions for the family. The family leaders called a family meeting. Together, the family scheduled a series of meetings over the next year and brought in skilled family coaches.

The family, as a unit, participated in these family meetings. They codeveloped the family values and a family wealth mission/purpose statement. We talk more about these processes in the next chapter.

Like most families, they were surprised to discover how many values were shared among their family members, even in the context of mistrust that permeated the gathered family. The family worked with the coaching team to build trust and communication skills within the family, dramatically improving their ability to talk with and support one another.

We compared the estate-planning documents, the family values, and their wealth mission to ensure that they were aligned. Using their newly learned communication skills, the family and advisors identified existing needs and developed the roles to fulfill those needs, along with the standards for qualification and performance (conditions of satisfaction for the roles).

The entire family worked its way through each of the processes, culminating in family members choosing the roles they were interested in and which best suited them. We analyzed their readiness, competencies, and qualifications. We developed individualized programs with implementation timelines and provided individual mentors.

After a concerted family effort on their own between family meetings, and in professional, well-run family meetings in a series of six two-day meetings over a twenty-month span, the post-coaching results showed remarkably improved results in each of the three areas measured. Trust and communication skills increased substantially, the family functioned more harmoniously, and disputes and family friction lessened. The overall assessment of the readiness of the family members was much improved – see comments from some family members on pages 75-76 as to their learning. This led to greater trust in the competencies of the next generation and the increased possibility of a stable succession and transition of wealth with a much lower likelihood of costly, post-transition disputes and possible litigation. The clarity of the family wealth mission/purpose was obvious to all and will serve as a compass for the family in the future.

"Eagle" Family Post-Coaching Graphs— 50-Question Survey Results

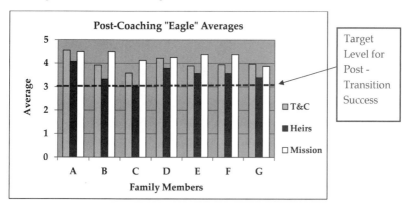

Summary of the Post-Coaching Report

The following conclusions are indicated after coaching.

This family has made remarkable progress and is clearly in the top 30 percent of families. They will likely experience a successful transition of wealth and succession.

This family scored well overall, with an average of 4.0 out of a perfect 5. Among the three major categories, at 3.5, Heir Readiness received the lowest overall score and merits further concentration.

Trust and Communication

The results in this category warrant an ongoing formal process within the family for communicating family estate, financial planning, asset management, and philanthropic endeavors (e.g., written, periodic scheduled family meetings with specific agenda items).

To further secure this successful transition, the family can productively spend time working on the following areas:

- Expanding their listening skills, internal communications, and communication effectiveness to ensure a more uniform understanding of who does what (now and especially in the future) and to ensure that the criteria for future planning decisions/changes are understood by all.

- Taking specific actions to further prepare family members to participate in the management of the family assets.

Heir Readiness

The family scored an average of 3.5 out of a perfect 5 in this category, indicating that most issues of heir preparation are being addressed. On the other hand, there was a variation of 33 percent in the individual family answers on this subject, which predicts a significant benefit if the topic of developing next-generation competencies is further addressed. Whether this is through the focused use of mentors or through making a range of possibilities available for family members to learn by managing family assets, this family needs to consider both.

Family Wealth Mission/Purpose Statement

This family averaged 4.2 out of a perfect 5 in this area. It is an indication that all members understand the family wealth mission/ purpose statement and understand that roles are being defined and redefined as needed. There remains some uncertainly about who is doing (or going to be doing) what. Each heir's specific future roles and responsibilities are worth reemphasis in the future. The minimal variance of 15 percent says that, for the most part, this area is converging squarely on target.

In chapters 7 and 8, we provide two more quizzes that are helpful to assess the family and individual family members' readiness.

Two elements required for the success of the process are:

(1) to acknowledge being a beginner

(2) to develop a family team

Being a Beginner—Developing Competence

The Williams Group Process introduces new communication skill sets and behaviors. It is essential to approach this work in a spirit of discovery and of being a beginner.

Often, individuals think they are expected to know or "should" know how to do something, even when they have never done it previously. When a family leader is open to learn, accepts that he or she is a beginner, and models behavior as a "beginner," it sets a new standard that such behavior is normal and unavoidable. Leaders who do this inspire acceptance of new learning within the rest of the family. We are all beginners at many times in our lives, and life is filled with the need for continual learning.

Running their enterprises, many family leaders become used to making many decisions quickly and are quick learners. In the business environment, it is often a more efficient use of a leader's time to hire someone already skilled to do something new rather than to have to take the time out to learn the skill personally. The family leader often develops excellent competence in managing people and processes at work, yet runs into difficulties in applying those same work competencies and processes in their family.

We are all beginners at many times in our lives, and life is filled with the need for continual learning.

As it relates to family, you cannot hire someone else to handle issues involving trust. The antecedents of establishing and maintaining trust need to be learned by the head family members and cannot be "contracted out" to someone else.

Becoming a Beginner—Roy Williams's Personal Experience

I will always remember the day I learned to be a beginner.

It occurred in a class on leadership. I had brought two coaches with me and paid a lot of money for the three of us to attend. There were approximately thirty people in the class. The instructor gave each of us three silk scarves and proceeded to show us how to juggle them.

Within just a few minutes, I had dropped the scarves many times and in frustration sat down, placing the scarves on the desk. The leader stated that according to his watch, I had attempted for three minutes before I sat down. He asked what the source of my frustration was. I told him I had spent a lot of money to be there, along with my coaches, and I had not come to learn scarf juggling.

The leader asked me, "What standard are you using that says within three minutes you are supposed to be minimally competent at juggling silk scarves?" Then he asked me, "Are you making an assessment that you should do it quickly because you are an ex-athlete?" He looked at my coaches, and they nodded their heads. He then made a statement that had a huge impact on me. He said, "Maybe if you would declare yourself a 'beginner,' you might learn faster."

Needless to say, I wanted to crawl under the desk. I cannot tell you how often I see people of all ages assume that because they are at a particular age or stage of life, they are supposed to know everything.

Declare yourself a beginner.

Accepting the role and label of a "beginner" is one of the first steps in learning and becoming a role model for all family members, thus making it easier for them to accept that it is normal to be a beginner. We were all beginners at many times in our lives and continue to be so. Family members need to become aware that life is filled with the need for continual learning.

Only when a current family leader is open to learn and accept that he or she is a beginner at something will that person become a role model and inspire acceptance of new learning among the family members. Some leaders, like me and many others, tend to be impatient and have difficulty accepting the reality of being a "beginner."

Learning is encouraged when family members feel comfortable in a role as a beginner and are not coerced into pretending to being skilled. Responsibility, given to family members without permission from the family leader to start the new task as a "beginner," is a fearful burden. The best offset to this fear is for the family leader to model be-

I cannot tell you how often I see people of all ages assume that because they are at a particular age or stage of life, they are supposed to know everything age-appropriate.

havior as a "beginner" and affirm that such behavior is normal and unavoidable. Actively being a beginner leads to confidence which leads to competence which leads to self esteem.

A graduate of a prominent business school had a six-inch spindle of unreturned phone messages on her desk as The Williams Group coach was interviewing her. When the coach asked about the work habits behind unreturned phone calls, the president of the company replied, "I just sold a bunch of my stock for fifty million dollars. I am ashamed to say that I don't know how to invest money...but I do know how to manage my company! So I had my secretary open FDIC-insured accounts in my name in different banks. Those banks are asking if I want to roll over the CDs. At least I won't lose anything!"

Initially she was unwilling to admit that she was a "beginner," and she was too embarrassed to ask for help at a task that she thought an MBA and CEO should know how to do. She decided to seek help from a professional coach. Over a period of six months, she learned how to select financial managers and hold them accountable for her fund performance—and returned her attention to running her company.

Being a Family Team

The American landscape is liberally sprinkled with fictionalized movie and book characters who purvey the false image of the "Savior Soldier" or "Lonesome Cowboy," who come individually to rescue the suffering. Movies dwell on the Lone Ranger theme, and announcers look for the MVP—(the most valuable player) of the game. The truth is, most successful achievements of almost any significance are the result of inspired, unified, and closely knit teams. Most of those teams respond to a shared mission and follow a leader who represents and adheres to their highest hopes and dreams. Abraham Lincoln, Mother Teresa, Nelson Mandela, Mahatma Gandhi, and Martin Luther King, Jr., are all great leaders of our time who inspired millions. Together they changed the world.

The ability to attain individual "heroism" is a false measure of anyone's competence.

A life well lived is a combination of experiences, thoughts, actions, and relationships. We are continually building and growing and learning. When we work with families, we see often that their togetherness as a unified family has been forgotten. When money becomes the focus in family meetings during wealth transition, there can be division and conflict. We work to get the families reconnected on a common goal of legacy and shared family values so they can become a team again. Peace and prosperity is right around the corner.

Teamwork is learned and is often not something people are raised with. I (Roy) learned teamwork participating in sports. I was always an athlete. Sports was my comfort zone in my youth. I learned how to work with others as a team and to take on specific roles on each team. Set goals, work hard, be disciplined, and know that just because you lost doesn't make you a loser.

When you are on a football team, you quickly learn that it takes others to play the game. You can't run the ball on your own. You don't throw a pass to yourself, and you can't make it to the end zone if someone doesn't have your back and block the players who are set on stopping you. You don't win alone, and you don't lose alone. You can't play and win at football if you're not part of a team. If you and the other players do not have the same values and goals based on trust, you will not remain on the team for the long term.

When I met my wife, she reinforced the importance of being a teammate and developing high trust. If you don't trust the people you are teamed up with, how you will you accomplish anything? There are few things in life you can do on your own. Most important decisions, activities, and relationships require teamwork. They require a collabo-

A life well lived is a combination of experiences, thoughts, actions, and relationships. We are continually building, growing, and learning.

ration with someone else to make it work. My wife showed me a different aspect of that trust and the way you work with someone as a team. It wasn't just sports at that point. It was a new way to look at being on a team and solving problems with someone.

Chapters 5, 6, and 7 provide in-depth information on forming a family team. Chapter 5 covers family meetings, chapter 6 covers coaching, and chapter 7 covers family philanthropy and preparing family members.

Chapter 4 Summary

As a result of research with thousands of affluent families and more than fifty-two years of working with these families, The Williams Group has developed a well-thought-out, tested, and proven measurable process and tools to identify the source of family conflict. We also have developed a clearly defined process to increase the odds substantially for a successful transition of financial wealth and family unity. Our method of pre- and post-analysis of the core drivers of successful family wealth transition show consistent improvement.

When family leaders begin to recognize the symptoms that threaten the harmony of the family and they are ready to take action to resolve it, the process begins with taking a closer look at the issues with an anonymous 50-Question Family Readiness Assessment. Then we generate a report from the responses of this analysis, and a coach presents it to the family. If the family decides to proceed with the next steps of the process, a coach will conduct confidential, individual interviews with each family member to understand the family and the family dynamics better. The family then creates a family meeting schedule.

In these family meetings, family members learn and

practice the skills to build trust and higher-level communication and relationship skills with real-life issues. The results are increased trust, new communication tools, and stronger, more sustainable levels of family unity and harmony. As a team, the family learns to resolve breakdowns, identify agreed-upon family values, and develop a shared mission for the family wealth and a glossary for clarity.

Developed from the agreed-upon family values, the Family Wealth Mission Statement becomes the compass for the family. We compare it with estate plans for alignment and use it to identify family needs that require roles. These processes are covered in-depth in the next chapter.

This invaluable information will help you think smarter about your wealth transition plan and complete the action steps you need to take to ensure a successful transition while retaining both financial and family assets.

CHAPTER

5

The Second Step: Securing Your Wealth Transition Plan

"Leadership has nothing to do with wealth and status, but is a matter of harmony."

—**Lao Tzu**

Experience has shown that family unity and harmony are essential for the successful transition of assets. Proactively rallying the family for the purpose of developing and acting on a well-thought-out plan of transition is one of the most welcome and bonding events a family experiences. A family's lack of preparation is the single largest risk to transitioning an estate.

We have found that proactively holding family meetings with a skilled coach who can provide direction, teach communication tools, and provide support and practice in real-life scenarios will substantially contribute toward preventing wealth-transfer failures. Throughout these processes, deep family bonding and commitment to the family values and to the family wealth mission/ purpose statement develops.

Focusing on a facilitated learning process during family meetings provides an opportunity for participation and growth for the entire family.

Family members who have had negative experiences and interactions with the family leaders exerting control in family meetings and in relationships often resist scheduling family meetings. These family members experience previous meetings as "lecture time" rather than "participation time." They may feel resentment or resignation and think that their participation will be unwelcome and that they will not have any influence in the decision-making processes. Until they experience a family meeting with skilled coaches, they are unable to see the value of these meetings.

As mentioned earlier, holiday events combined with family meetings, before trust and communication skills have been developed, often result in high levels of stress and anxiety prior to and throughout the holiday. These meetings leave family members with bad memories and fail to accomplish the desired goals. It is not uncommon for family members to walk on eggshells, hoping to avoid setting anyone off, looking for others to validate negative assessments, and talking about each other rather than to each other.

Family meetings can be held effectively during a gathering period (holidays, birthdays) when held separate from the celebratory gathering itself and guided by a professional coach.

The best results happen when family meetings involve the entire family, including spouses and significant others, and are an integrative process based on open, clear, and authentic communication. Everyone is sought out for thoughts, opinions, and recommendations. For some family members, it is the first time they experience their voice being heard. The family meetings begin as two-day affairs, with absolute confidentiality maintained within the family. The family leaders make strong efforts to ensure that all family members attend and are heard.

Many families choose to hold their meetings at a spa or resort facility and build in fun, learning, and replenishing activities as a family around the meetings. These families come to look forward to the family's time together—even those family members who initially thought they could not carve two days out of their lives and those who were concerned about having to deal with family tensions.

The Value of Family Meetings

The physical contact and presence with family members that occurs in family meetings is vital in building the family as a team. In one particular family, they had never all come together for the sake of discussing the family and its relationship to each other and to their wealth. Although they all lived in the same area, and had generally good relationships with each other, they never all sat down together to discuss their family identity. The moment everyone settled into their chairs, there was a palpable sense of unity, so much so that a few family members were moved to tears. It was the first time they had acknowledged they are a family. Taking the action to all come together galvanized

For some family members, it is the first time they experience their voice being heard.

their commitment to strengthening family relationships. One family member remarked that he never felt the family was a team before. He said he used to go to his friend's house to experience what it felt like to be in a "normal" family.

Time spent during the family meeting developing the family values and developing the family wealth mission/purpose statement based upon those values, builds new levels of intimacy, trust, and communication between all family members. While the end product of a family wealth mission/purpose statement provides the compass and keel of the family, the process to that outcome is often where the true learning and value is generated.

Feedback from a Few Family Meetings

(Shared with permission of the family members without name identifiers.)

"I was satisfied with our discussions and interactions. Although I was initially resistant, I am grateful to my very busy family for making this happen. I am impressed at how quickly we all became engaged, listened, and learned. I can't remember spending two days in this kind of engagement with anyone."

"I found the meetings very productive. This is the first time I feel like we are a family."

"We covered a lot of ground yesterday. Even though I felt uncomfortable at first, I learned about myself and from the experience."

> *The moment everyone settled into their chairs, there was a palpable sense of unity, so much so that a few family members were moved to tears.*

"I appreciate that the other half of the family is not trying to screw us. I tend to automatically think that is the case. I just need to be reminded that they have their problems and bring a little empathy to their situation."

"I appreciate that we have come a long way. Our communication is much better. These times together allow us to get back on track and be a family."

"When we have a family meeting, we address underlying issues and focus on each of us individually and as a family, instead of focusing on logistics and technical aspects of the family business."

"I am very glad we all made the effort to get together to do this. You guys know what you are doing. I've been impressed repeatedly. There have been a number of high points. I like learning. I have less uncertainty regarding my future and feel less overwhelmed by my obligations."

"Now I want to put myself in situations where I am pressing myself, and I am feeling a sense of achievement."

"I found the request circle a helpful way to interact. I never consciously thought about asking for understanding of all the details. Now I feel empowered to decline some requests." (A request circle is a tool The Williams Group uses to help families make clear requests.)

"I will be more open to how I am feeling and when I am out of my comfort zone. After the first day, I became more comfortable with being in discovery; it took a great deal of openness to do the last exercise."

"I liked the in-person conversations. While I was growing up, we did not have open communication, and to my surprise I very much enjoyed the in-person conversations."

"Some of this I already knew and could not share with my family—and now I can. I liked getting into assessments and assertions early."

"We had fun conversations on a variety of topics last night. I like practicing different conversations in a safe environment."

During family meetings, trust and communication tools are taught and practiced throughout the process.

Trust

Trust is the Golden Thread That Holds Families Together

What does trust mean to you? What is the trust level in your family?

Trust and communication are the foundations for a unified family. In the context of The Williams Group Process and this book, when we write about trust we are not referring to avoiding fraud, dishonesty, purposeful deceit, or illegal activity. We are talking about the components of trust[13] made up of genuine care (which eliminates the possibility of the actions just mentioned). These three major components are present in family members who trust one another:

- **Reliability**—Family members do what they say they will do, when they promised to do it.

- **Sincerity**—An individual's internal story matches his or her external story. They mean what they say.

- **Competence**—The individual has the ability, skill, and capacity to accomplish and meet commitments he or she makes. For example, the eldest son may not have the appropriate skill set to be the executor.

All three components must be present in a caring environment for authentic trust among individuals to exist. This enables family members to accept the risk of betrayal or failure, accept that a breach of trust was unintentional, and accept efforts made to repair the breach. Without trust, there is little to no authentic communication, and in most cases, not even any desire or interest in communicating. Trust is the root of relationships.

One cause of a loss of trust results is repeated failures to live up to promises. Promising to be home for dinner, at the recital, at the parent-teacher meeting, or at the basketball game, and then frequently failing to show up or arriving late, establishes a pattern of negative expectations and leads to a reputation of untrustworthiness and unreliability.

Trust and communication are the foundations for a unified family.

---

13. Robert Solomon and Dr. Fernando Flores, *Building Trust* (New York: Oxford University Press, 2001), 134.

Leslie had a history of not turning up for pre-arranged meetings with his children. He was a busy executive, running a very large enterprise with six corporate presidents reporting to him. His children loved him and wanted to be with him. They came to believe that his priorities were money and business and that they and the family were unimportant. Those thoughts negatively impacted their self-esteem. Dad had a different perspective. He was committed to working hard and long hours to build his company for his children. He thought they should appreciate, understand, and be grateful for his focus on making money for the family.

He frequently committed to attending functions or doing activities with the children or family, and then a business opportunity or problem would arise. His continual unreliability in fulfilling his commitments to the family (other than money) sent them an unintended message. One of his daughters stated that she did not trust her dad. She recounted a story, which she added was one of many similar stories, about having an agreement with her dad to meet him at his office for lunch one afternoon. She was very excited and looking forward to having this time with her dad. She waited and waited. After more than an hour, her father's assistant apologized to her, saying her dad had been called to a meeting and would not be back till much later.

In the family meeting, she shared this memory with her dad. He could not hear her without numerous attempts and the assistance of a coach. When he could take it in, he apologized and made a commitment to track his commitments with her. It took three years of rigorous record keeping of his promises and fulfilling these promises to get his children to believe he had become trustworthy (reliable). As a consequence of his diligence with his children, his six corporate presidents also noted his increased reliability at work.

Most parents are absolutely sincere when they promise to be at the soccer game or whatever event is important to their child. They certainly are competent in terms of entering the date and time into their schedules. If they repeatedly miss making it to events, their lack of reliability erodes trust within the family, and they unwittingly end up role-modeling unreliability.

At the very least, it is critical to inform children ahead of time when it becomes apparent that a family leader will be unable to maintain his or her commitment (managing their commitment). While it is understood that most parents are doing their level best to generate wealth for the family, and often for philanthropic reasons, simultaneously they are challenged with how to balance work and family. When one succeeds at this, it is most rewarding to the entire family.

Developmentally a young child cannot relate to their physician mother being called in for another emergency. The message received by the children is that they are less important than almost anything else and that their parent cannot be

> *Simply knowing the right steps is a far cry from doing the right steps.*

relied upon. Their disappointment turns into anger, resentment, and ultimately disengagement.

Teaching, practicing, and testing the required skills for trust and communication have turned out to be much more important skills than any of the researchers had initially forecasted; it is critical for the practice to take place within the family environment on real issues. Once the leaders of the family understand what skill sets are required, they set about learning, practicing, modeling, and encouraging family members to do the same.

They understand that simply *knowing* the right steps is a far cry from *doing* the right steps. It's like dancing. In the dance studio, the steps might be painted on the floor, and everyone might agree that those steps are accurate in describing the dance. But actually dancing with one another is an entirely different skill. *Practice* is the point in the learning process where knowledge and skill are integrated and applied. We say learning has happened when a family member can take new action and have conversations turn out in a way that promotes trust and understanding.

Communication

"Seek first to understand, then to be understood."
—**Steven Covey,** *The 7 Habits of Highly Effective People*

Most of our communication habits are unconsciously inherited. We learn to communicate through our parents' modeling, and they learned from their parents. These communication styles, healthy or not, are the water we swim in without being aware of the water. There comes a time when those communication habits are no longer effective in navigating the complex conversations of increasing wealth or growing modern families.

Learning has happened when a family member can take new action.

Listening is a learned skill, needs to be practiced, and it is the most important skill requirement for effective communication. *Listening does not equal hearing.* Listening requires being able to be fully present with the speaker; and to be able to paraphrase; to speak openly, honestly, respectfully, and freely concerning information sought by other family members. The purpose of this type of listening is to obtain an understanding of the other person and to comprehend his or her point of view instead of listening to reply, refute or defend. When challenging communications occur, we often form a reply in our minds instead of listening, which results in reacting instead of responding. Listening requires setting our own thoughts/agenda aside and hearing the speaker's interpretation, not just our own.

Listening does not equal hearing.

Learning to ask questions is a vital communication skill to gain understanding of other's perceptions. In some families, people avoid asking questions out of fear of reaction or fear of being perceived as prying, inappropriate, or less than. To be effective, communication requires a foundation of authentic trust. These skills unify the family for common action and shared responsibilities and to resolve past misunderstandings or disagreements.

There are numerous interpretations of the word "communication." Basically, it is a two-way process of exchanging information, news, ideas, and feelings to reach a mutual understanding and shared meaning in an effort to create connection. One interpretation includes common action—we communicate to achieve common action.

Reaching common understanding and a commitment to common action helps to keep the family aligned with the family wealth mission/purpose statement; reinforces family unity; and avoids wasting time, energy, and money on disputes resulting from separate action or no action at all. Communication breakdowns among family members results in divisions that can lead to family members being skeptical of others' intentions and can lead to family members taking separate actions that result in disputes and even litigation.

Listening requires setting our own thoughts/ agenda aside and hearing the speaker's interpretation, not just our own.

Trust and communication improve remarkably as a result of well-run and professionally led family meetings in which issues around breakdowns in trust and communication can be addressed and remedies practiced within the family.

"The truth is that our finest moments are most likely to occur when we are feeling deeply uncomfortable, unhappy, or unfulfilled. For it is only in such moments, propelled by our discomfort, that we are likely to step out of our ruts and start searching for different ways or truer answers."
—M. Scott Peck

Cordial Hypocrisy

We believe it is essential to engage in some of the "missing" conversations before deeper levels of trust can be built. Without first learning how to engage in those more challenging conversations in productive ways, cordial hypocrisy will rule the nature of conversations. We have consistently observed that communication often leans towards cordial hypocrisy, which is a way of relating that lacks authenticity. We all do it from time to time, whether it's at the Christmas dinner with the dysfunctional aunt who is merely tolerated or within the family feud that's ignored. Avoiding conflict becomes paramount, and communication is sanitized.

We have consistently observed that communication often leans towards cordial hypocrisy, which is a way of relating that lacks authenticity.

Cordial hypocrisy is a process whereby people accept what they don't want to accept in favor of avoiding rocking the boat. When the family leaders explore previously avoided discussions, they help put a stop to cordial hypocrisy. It is necessary to model this behavior. Failure to do so will result in continued cordial hypocrisy and meaningless "lip service."

Looking at your communications with family members, do you recognize any cordial hypocrisy?

Perception

"Two people can see the same thing, disagree, and yet both be right. It's not logical; it's psychological... We see the world, not as it is, but as we are or, as we are conditioned to see it."
—**Steven Covey**

Yet another challenging aspect of communication is perception. The speaker and the listener may have two completely different perspectives on the issue being discussed.

You may perceive a gesture as insulting in your country, while someone from another country and culture may be intending you to perceive the gesture as helpful! If I trust that you are trying to help me, I will raise the question when some communication is so obviously out of sync with our conversation and declared intentions. Large discrepancies are easy to detect, while subtle ones often pass undetected and eventually accumulate into a major misunderstanding. The issue of differing perceptions and breakdowns in trust are responsible for most communication failures.

The way people view the following diagram is a great example of how differing perspectives can cloud communications.

When people in North America view this picture, they see a side of a building with a window and three stick people either inside or outside. In rural Kenya, people see a tree denuded by elephants and giraffes and a woman carrying a package to market with two others.

The North Americans' perception and the Kenyans' perception are what they are, based on their history. The point is that a breakdown of communication may be a fundamental perception issue. Imagine if your family were viewing a trust document instead of a picture of stick figures. The difference in interpretation could have significant consequences. Listening to understand rather than to be understood helps reveal underlying perceptions, which leads to clearer communication.

Family Values, a Wealth Mission Statement, and Consensus Building

Once the family has learned and practiced tools for effective communication and trust, coaches support the family in continuing to practice these tools to identify agreed-upon family values and to develop the Family Wealth Mission Statement that defines the long-term purpose of the family wealth. Underlying issues that prevent authentic trust and honest communication must be addressed before the values and mission can be established. If cordial hypocrisy continues to pervade the culture of the family, there will be insufficient buy-in to the Family Wealth Mission Statement. The values and mission will lay on a strong foundation of family relationships and engagement once the barriers to trust have been addressed.

Often, by the time a family comes together to discuss their values and mission statement, the children are adults and have families of their own.

The family develops a glossary of each word used in the family wealth mission/purpose statement to clarify the family's intentions, and to guide their professional advisors. Graphic illustrators create a chart of family values and of the family wealth mission/purpose statement for the family, which most families frame and hang where meetings are held. This is part of an overarching, proven process that will keep everyone on target. It translates their individual wishes into a consensus, leading to specific estate instructions and actions, all while building a family team. An additional value of the process is in the road map that is created through the alignment and shared vision of all family members.

True family wealth is very evident when we sit down and coach families through the process of articulating their values and determining what practices they have in their lives because of those values. A safe space is created that is marked by generous listening as each person shares what matters to him or her and what he or she deeply cares about. Family members have the opportunity to formulate their thoughts, be heard and supported, and reach alignment. The process produces a sense of intimacy and connection, and it brings clarity and acceptance to the diversity in the family.

Often, by the time a family comes together to discuss their values and mission statement, the children are adults and have families of their own. They believe they have their own set of values and are not always sure the larger family shares the same values, or even respects theirs. We see this represented in subtle judgments about how a particular family raises its children, or in instances where the tolerance granted to one sibling is markedly different than that granted to another.

When a family engages in the process of defining their values, they are often both relieved and astounded by how many values they hold in common. Having the freedom to express their individual values in the key areas of life in a trusting environment and engaging in conversations about them allows the amalgamation to evolve.

Gratitude is the doorway to happiness and peace.

From this process, the family moves into codesigning a family wealth mission/purpose statement. Doing so provides a more expansive, loving, and inclusive model for all family members to connect to.

Once family members connect on the agreed-upon family values and their co-created family wealth mission/purpose statement, the family becomes a family team with a compass and a keel that all family members can refer to when making decisions. A family wealth mission/purpose statement provides family members with a deep sense of family and a commitment to ensure that the wealth transition is a positive and sustainable experience that extends into future generations.

Through these processes the mood of the family changes to one of appreciation and gratitude, and gratitude is the doorway to happiness and peace. Throughout these processes the family members are becoming skilled communicators.

Master coaches are very skilled in this well-thought-out, tried, and tested process, which The Williams Group developed over decades of working directly with families to prepare their wealth transfer and their heirs proactively. Family members easily relate to the coaches and the process, and they learn together. After practice in real family situations, they integrate the learned skills into their families and lives.

A family wealth mission/purpose statement provides guidance to the professionals; enables them to provide solutions more efficiently; and enables them to coordinate their legal, accounting, and investment efforts more coherently. The wealth mission statement is vital in creating a bridge between the family values and estate documents. It also provides professionals with an essential agreed-upon reference framework for all major issues.

Without a consensus on the long-term mission for the family wealth, the default focus for professionals is wealth preservation, taxation minimization, and governance/control - these three elements are not the cause of the 70 percent failure rate of estate transitions.

Families who lack agreed-upon family values and a wealth mission statement based on these values run the risk of wealth-transition failure. The involvement of the entire family from around age sixteen in the decision-making process is one of the key factors in successful family wealth transitions. Although more difficult and time consuming, it avoids the trap of Mom or Dad attempting to dictate "the future" to

The wealth mission statement is vital in creating a bridge between the family values and estate documents.

their children. Parents who make unilateral decisions regarding future generations and the transitioning of the estate are neither effective nor unifying. One of our family leaders said, "To do so is sowing the seeds of destruction."

Our research suggests that parents accept the input of their heirs on the parents' decisions. This does not mean parents yield authority or control. It does mean giving information to heirs, allowing heirs to offer input and influence on major transition decisions, and receiving their input with respect and consideration.

In the event that Mom or Dad privately decides (even together) what is to be done with the financial assets, their deaths often result in open disagreement among the siblings. Siblings often hold their own opinions about what should be done with the financial assets and/or family business. They may resent that they were excluded from decisions that impacted them and their futures. This can cause a split in generational unity. While great authority is held by the leaders of a family who owns/controls the family business or wealth while they are living, it is naïve to believe this authority can be projected into the future reliably.

Failing to prepare family members for succession and wealth transfer proactively can result in a lack of agreement among siblings. Without preparation, often the only unifying factor of the siblings is sharing the legal expenses of getting the will overturned or the trust agreement broken. (They usually reach quick agreement that family funds can be used to rewrite the edicts of a departed Mom and/or Dad or for litigation.) In short, it appears unrealistic for parents to expect that they can direct the priorities of their family members or future generations based on documents developed privately with legal counsel.

The Garen family had reached agreement on the family values and created a family wealth mission/purpose statement together. After four family meetings, they invited the professional advisors to join a family meeting to design a strategy and structure to accomplish the family wealth mission/purpose. They wanted the new plan to enable their account to grow and to preserve the wealth while minimizing taxes.

With a competent family coach, the meeting began at 9:00 a.m. with the family's instructions that, by day's end, they wanted a wealth-transition plan. The professionals were mandated to reach an agreement, that same day, on the outline of a plan that would fulfill the family mission. This was a first for the attorneys, accountants, and tax, insurance, and financial advisors—to reach consensus with the entire family in the design of a strategy and structure to accomplish the family wealth mission/purpose. At the end of the day, a plan outline was delivered. All family members and advisors agreed on the plan. The advisors completed the detailed documents within thirty days. The family team had mastered the dance.

Here are just some of the benefits that result for the family and their professional advisors when the wealth mission/purpose statement is written and built through a consensus process:

- Family members agree with the long-term mission of the family wealth.

- There is less ambiguity in questions about the distribution schemes and how governance, preservation, and tax issues are to be addressed.

- The family is able to make a more rapid assessment of how changes in the tax law impact the family transition plan. Rapid changes in documents can be made based, on the family wealth mission/purpose statement, not solely to reduce or avoid taxes.

- Family conflict issues that arise can be correlated with the family wealth mission/purpose statement to provide clarification and help resolve issues more rapidly and accurately.

- It creates a platform for transferring values into action through financial plans, philanthropic activities, and individual career goals.

- It creates a conduit for transferring values to the next generation through the definitions in the glossary.

- It develops trust and communication skills within the family.

Four brothers who were in business together were our clients. Because of the natural stresses of owning and managing a company together, and also being a family, they had developed a pattern of communication that lacked sincerity because of their efforts to avoid conflict over the years.

The youngest brother often replied favorably to suggestions from the other brothers, even though he didn't agree with the suggestions at all; then he would ignore their suggestions. Another resented one of his brothers for what he perceived as his authoritarian decision making. The lack of authenticity among the brothers resulted in cordial hypocrisy and resentment. Their level of connection was growing more distant as time went on. Finally, one of the brothers hired an attorney to negotiate an exit strategy aimed at getting him the most he could out of the business and thus compromise the ability of the business to continue.

Once the family members developed their communication skills and began to create solid trust with each other, they were able to speak more openly in ways they had thought impossible previously. Their initial concerns when they came to The Williams Group revealed frustrations with how they communicated with each other about the business, as well as with their wives and children. During the third family meeting, they began to have meaningful family dialogue.

As they progressed through The Williams Group Process, they all learned how to express themselves more genuinely and greatly minimized their fear of conflict. During the process, the coaches supported the family in cocreating their values chart and the family wealth mission/purpose statement. This helped ensure that the family was aligned on the direction and goal of the family wealth.

Now they function as a high-performing team; their relationships with their wives are no longer conflicted by unresolved family business decisions, and they are more congruent. The brothers report that they have been able to use the skills learned, and it has resulted in all their partnerships being much more authentic and fluid.

Chapter 5 Summary

In this chapter, we presented tools to enable families to achieve family unity and harmony, which is one-half of the wealth equation. To ensure a successful transfer of assets from one generation to the next, the family is called to address both the financial and the family unity aspects proactively by giving each the time, energy, and attention they require and deserve. Historically, the aspect that has received the most attention is the creation and transfer of financial assets.

Well-documented evidence shows that the greatest threat to a successful wealth transfer lies with a poorly prepared family prior to the transfer taking place.

One of the three issues that undermines a successful transfer of wealth is a breakdown of trust and communication within the family unit, weighted 60 percent in succession failures. Once the issues behind the distrust have been addressed, then the family values and mission statement can be cocreated. These breakdowns can be navigated with coach facilitation in family meetings, and the family can acquire and practice new trust and communication skills. These skills are then used to identify agreed-upon family values and to develop a Family Wealth Mission Statement that becomes the family's compass for future decision-making. At the same time, an authentic family team is being developed and unified.

It is helpful to be aware that perceptions and cordial hypocrisy influence communications. Listening for understanding is an essential communication and relationship building skill. The Williams Group Process and our coaches teach these life-enhancing skills, keep the decision-making moving ahead, prevent important issues from being ignored for fear of conflict, and require the participants practice what they have agreed to.

CHAPTER

6

The Third Step: Turning Transition Deficiencies into an Action Plan for Success

The greatest danger in times of turbulence is not the turbulence; it is to act with yesterday's logic."

—Peter Drucker

Embracing Change to Start New Action

Fly fishermen don't rely on the same fly for every fish. Hunters don't always wait in the same location. Businesspeople don't run the same advertisements ad infinitum, even if past advertisements have been successful. Change is essential to remain competitive and to sustain vitality in an ever-changing environment. Similarly, successful succession and wealth transfers demand adapting to the changing lives of everyone involved.

We become comfortable in known environments and rely

on repetitive situations to leverage our personal strengths. In fact, we unconsciously "fortify" our environment and processes against outside disruption, all in the name of "comfort" or "focus." Our identities are intimately connected to our surroundings, roles, and relationships. This desire for comfort can also result in a desire to avoid planning for succession and wealth transfers that involve a future change in our position of authority, and therefore our identity. This type of planning requires navigating relationships that may have become tense or even conflicted. It makes most people uncomfortable because it demands skills they may not have developed yet. This goes back to learning to be a beginner, which we talked about in chapter 4.

There is intrinsic satisfaction and enjoyment in learning, having new experiences, and designing a plan for the future. Despite this, people often resist change. Change can be uncomfortable and requires that we leave our comfort zones to grow. We live in an ever-changing world, and when we embrace change, it can be exhilarating and move us to a new and higher level of functioning. In today's globally aware, ever-changing world, the constant need to adapt and reinvent ourselves requires the qualities of adaptability, flexibility, and resilience, which are understandably in high demand and highly valued.

Usually, in midlife, leaders and parents begin (quietly and privately) planning a peaceful and "fair" distribution of the fruits of their lifetime of effort with the help of their trusted lawyer, accountant, and estate planner or investment advisor. At first, many parents find it uncomfortable to talk with their children

There is intrinsic satisfaction and enjoyment in learning, having new experiences, and designing a plan for the future.

about their thinking, their personal plans, and their concerns for each of the children. Evidence shows that this way of dealing with succession needs to change. The easier decision to avoid involving the entire family (for scheduling or other reasons) has proved consistently harmful to successful family transition planning.

Few changes in a person's life, especially a child's life, are as challenging as the sudden responsibility of wealth transferred from a recently departed parent or grandparent. The magnitude of the loss concurrently results in a powerful, and in some instances, an overwhelming impact. Unwittingly parents frequently compound this substantive change by having decided the wealth transition in isolation from the children.

Family members' lack of preparation is a great risk to the successful transitioning of an estate. Preparing family members begins with the entire family resolving breakdowns in trust and communication, identifying the family values, developing a family wealth mission/purpose statement, and proactively preparing family members to be accountable and responsible. Unless these steps are undertaken, the distribution of family wealth can result in unplanned, toxic ramifications, which can include discord, disputes, family feuds, and litigation.

Once the family leader(s) self-assess their potential for a successful estate transition (the ten questions in chapter 3), they generally find themselves feeling like this:

- Grateful for knowing where they stand

- Concerned about the low odds of success

- Curious about how to begin making the needed changes

Some families who do this preliminary assessment of their estate transition status find the score they received unsettling. The answers may predict that unless they initiate and follow through with implementing changes, the odds of a successful estate transition are in the 30 percent range. Unless they create a proactive cooperative learning environment for the next generation, the chance of failure increases. It is only a 9 percent success rate by the third generation (30 percent x 30 percent = 9 percent), hence the term "shirtsleeves-to-shirtsleeves in three generations." If the family chooses to make the call for changes, they can move the odds up into the 70 to 90 percent range! How is this accomplished?

Increasing the odds of a successful wealth transfer is accomplished by focusing on preparing family members through the family meetings. The goal is for them to learn the skill sets needed to develop trust and communication and to use these skills to participate in the following processes:

- Navigating important repressed conversations

- Identifying family values

- Developing a family wealth mission to serve as their compass and keel

- Gaining understanding of the estate plans

- Comparing the estate plans and family wealth mission for congruency

- Identifying the needs and the roles to fulfill those needs

- Developing the qualifications, experience requirements, and performance standards of satisfaction for each role

- Identifying the roles they wish to fill

- Making a plan and timeline to qualify for the role

Increasing the odds of a successful wealth transfer is accomplished by focusing on preparing family members through the family meetings and making commitments.

In the previous chapter, we covered in-depth the value of identifying family values and developing a family wealth mission/purpose statement. The next step in preparing family members is to provide them with an understanding of the estate plans and then to compare the estate plans with the family wealth mission/purpose statement for congruency. The family, with coaching support and participation from the financial and legal team, identifies any unmet needs of the family, creates roles to meet these needs, and develops qualifications and performance standards of satisfaction for each role.

All the Stanley family members, including grandchildren age sixteen and older, participated in developing "Inheritance Standards." The resulting wills and estate documents stated, "The children must be employed five years prior to receiving any financial distribution, and they must have received increased work responsibility and be paid accordingly. If they fail to achieve these standards, they have one more five-year time period to meet the employment-promotion requirement, and if they cannot, the funds will revert to the family foundation."

The parents were delighted by the family-wide support for the development and acceptance of the proposed standards.

These steps in the process provide yet another opportunity for the family to use their evolving trust and communication skill sets while building more trust and bonding the family unit even more firmly.

Inevitably, conflicts exist between the estate planning documents developed by the estate planning team, and the family values and family wealth mission/purpose developed by the entire family. These conflicts arise because the family wealth mission/purpose is about what is important to the entire family and how they wish their wealth to be directed, and the estate plans are about strategy and structure wrapped around governance, preservation, and tax-reduction techniques covering assets.

When comparing these documents, the issue of *fair versus equal* arises for consideration and discussion. The family wealth mission/purpose statement frequently declares a commitment to treating everyone equally. On the other hand, the will may say, for example, that one child who works in the business will receive a larger percentage of the distributions. Estate documents may state that trusts can be accessed for health and welfare, as they typically do, and the family wealth mission/purpose statement may declare education as an important value to keep alive. Consequently, the family member who wants to access his or her "trust for educational purposes" can be denied.

Another typical example of the disconnect between estate documents and family wealth mission/purpose is the family's expressed commitment during the development of the family wealth mission/purpose statement to keep all family members informed of changes and connected to each other as the family and business grows. To fulfill this identified need, it might be necessary to create a role to establish a family council. This council may also establish protocol for the next generation entering the business and to decide how ownership will be determined and how distributions will be calculated. The family may need to modify estate documents to invest and give the family council the authority and power required to implement the needs of the growing family.

In some instances, when developing the qualifications and experience requirements, individuals already in a role may realize that they need more qualifications and/or experience. Other individuals choose the role they want to fill and design a plan and a timeline to acquire the qualifications and experience to fill the role. This is usually a very exciting and uplifting process for the entire family. When family members become involved and active in these processes and set goals, the family leaders are reassured that their lifetime of work is in good hands.

Family involvement in developing the qualifications and experience requirements and performance standards helps all family members recognize the importance of family members developing competency and self-confidence, which results in healthy self-esteem. Along with developing self-confidence, the trust among the next generation is deepened as they all have a clear and mutual understanding of the shared standards for success in key roles such as head of the family council, trustee, financial and investment advisors, or even beneficiary. If no family member wishes to fill a role, the qualification and experience requirements are used to hire an outside party.

This is an excellent opportunity for the family leaders to share how they decide the competence level of the advisors they surround themselves with. Learning to assess the skills of key advisors is an important skill to pass along to the next generation. The family leader in this instance has an opportunity to educate future generations on how to avoid the pitfalls of expensive mistakes at the hands of unqualified, incompetent, or untrustworthy advisors. It can be a powerful conversation that gives the next generation the opportunity to learn how to build a team from a successful business leader.

Some of the qualities we have heard family leaders say they look for in advisors are as follows:

- They are team players who are willing to consult with other advisors.

- They have sound investment philosophies.

- Their fee structure is clear, with no surprises.

- The referral source is reputable.

- Their references say they are trustworthy – reliable, sincere and competent.

- They have a large network.

- They use specific and measurable standards to know if they are doing a good job.

- They return calls within twenty-four hours.

Learning to assess the skills of key advisors is an important skill to pass along to the next generation.

The family wealth mission/purpose often calls for philanthropic action. If the family does not already have a philanthropic focus, the family may decide, with the assistance of the attorney and financial advisors, to create a foundation or philanthropic arm. Once again, needs and roles will be identified, and qualification and performance standards developed. Philanthropy and its relationship to family members will be covered in depth in chapter 7.

When business owners reach conclusions about their products, they act with deliberate haste. If the product is faulty, they withdraw it; if materials become illegal, ineffective, or unavailable, the owners recall or replace them. If the contract is lost, they replace it with a new sales effort. If imported raw materials become limited, the owners initiate a change in process, pricing, or supplier. Everyone adjusts to the task of correcting the situation as soon as possible. The US Navy refers to this total response as "General Quarters." When the ship's alarm sounds "General Quarters," every able-bodied member of the crew responds to emergency stations, ready for priority responsibilities and additional duties as necessary. The resources are rallied, and action is taken. The life of the ship is critical to the life of its crew, cargo, and mission.

Sometimes focus is placed on continuing to generate more wealth at the expense of preparing the family.

Dealing with family issues that threaten the orderly transition of family wealth and responsibility is equally critical. It is a matter of rallying the family and outside resources to address the largest risk of all: the risk that the hard-won family estate may fail to transition successfully, resulting in family discord. We encourage families to develop a strategic and tactical plan to ensure a successful wealth transition. When the family leadership initiates and commits to the steps necessary to prepare their family for a successful transition, it is a signal to the entire family that they have decided to address the challenges everyone knows are present in a proactive way. It's also a call to action for all family members.

Given that a change in responsibility is inevitable (people are born, marry, and die), our research kept encouraging us to ask the question, "Why is the preparation for family members so casual, unstructured, and often considered 'optional?'" The key factor appears to be that the focus is placed on continuing to generate more wealth at the expense of preparing the family. Once the family members' lack of preparation is acknowledged, whether the preparation is done well or poorly, expertise and commitment are required. Successful families frequently obtain outside support in the form of a mentor or family coach. This outside, specialized assistance is in addition to the legal/accounting/financial management advisors the family routinely uses. The family leadership selects an appropriate coach for the family's needs to aid them in their transition planning process.

How Can My Family Select a Family Coach?

To prepare family members and work with family systems requires coaches who are skilled practitioners, evolved from other professional fields, with years of experience in the coaching domain. The coach may have previously been a psychologist, an estate planner, a social worker, an educator, or someone in the communication field. When we reviewed the research results to compare families who successfully transitioned their wealth versus those who did not, certain competencies of the family coaches who worked with the families began to surface.

We encourage families to develop a strategic and tactical plan to ensure a successful wealth transition based on trust and communication.

Every Williams Group family meeting has one Lead Coach and one Listening Coach. Also available are specialty coaches who might join the advising team, depending on the family's needs:

- Role Development Coach
- Passion Coach
- Implementation Coach

Our coaches have been trained in developing high-performing teams in families and organizations with a specific emphasis on how language and mood affect coordination of the planning effort. Let's look at the roles of our coaches.

Lead Coach—Our lead coaches are our most experienced. Each has a minimum of fifteen years of coaching experience in families and organizations. They are responsible for facilitating meaningful conversations, teaching the relevant communication tools at the right time, and ensuring the overall success of the family experience.

Listening Coach—Our listening coaches are expert listeners. They are trained to listen for what is being said as well as what is not being said, when to explore a particular topic further, and to ensure that the important topics are brought to the surface during family meetings. A primary role for the listening coach is to establish an atmosphere of safety and trust.

Role Development Coach—This specialized coach is charged with identifying the multiple needs and roles based on the family's values and mission that were developed earlier in the process and their estate plans. Just a few examples of such roles include executor, trustee, family office executive, money manager, and foundation head. Each role requires observable and measurable standards for qualification and performance. This includes the roles of all professional advisors in case any of the family advisors can no longer fill the role, necessitating the hiring of a new advisor. The advisor will have helped develop the standards to replace him/herself. When this process includes the family, the advisors, and any person who helps identify the needs and roles, it deepens the knowledge, builds the entire team, and becomes a model for future generations to use.

Passion Coach—Typically the passion coach works with the next generation to identify their passions. At times they will work with the current family leader(s) to begin to explore the next stage of their career as they make room for the next generation to take roles they want and are prepared for. The passion coach may use networking strategies, one-on-one coaching, interviews with other family members, and shadowing techniques, among other strategies, to support a family member in identifying his or her next role and life's passion.

Implementation Coach—An implementation coach works closely with the family in implementing its Family Wealth Mission Statement. This coach works with the family to identify educational needs, governance, investment strategies, and philanthropic goals. He or she also works closely with the family advisors and may come from the legal, accounting, or tax fields.

All successful coaches will have the following identifiable characteristics:

1. They are nonjudgmental and independent.

2. They are committed to the best outcome for the family.

3. They have no conflicts of financial interest.

4. They have developed a consistent process and can explain the process in a manner that is easy to understand.

5. They build skills with family members in areas necessary for a successful transition of family wealth. They do not stop their work once a solution is found but instead continue their work until the family is proficient in the skills required to implement and maintain the solution.

6. They have a "track record" of working with successful families who are willing to serve as a reference for them and their process.

7. The coach is part of a larger team with a spectrum of resources to draw from.

Other coach characteristics, such as age, gender, and length of time in the field all relate more closely to the overall family comfort level, especially with the patriarch and matriarch leaders.

The process of preparing the next generation requires family leadership, trust within the family; a committed family team; and an assembly of experts in relationship building, communication, business, philanthropy, investments, and estate planning. Each specialty requires specific, well-developed skills. As mentioned earlier, good relationship and communication skills are foundational and critical to the long-term growth and success of a family. Often master coaches are required. They are skilled in assisting with the breakdowns that occur within families and can support the family to learn new ways to navigate challenging communication issues. As parents, we often discover we are unable to coach our own family members. Recall attempting to teach your own children to drive!

Estate planning professionals and financial advisors view effective coaching of the family as a "value add" that can reduce the cost of other long-term professional assistance. Another valuable outcome we see in our research is that through the planning process, families come to understand the importance of accountability, qualifications, experience, and performance standards (conditions of satisfaction) and feel more qualified to select and evaluate professionals to assist the family in other matters.

What Are the Signs of a Well-Coached Family?

This is a question several families have asked us. They want to visualize their "after" picture as well as their "before" picture. For the most part, our answer is simple. A well-coached family with accompanying high odds of a successful wealth transition exhibits these qualities:

- There are no "taboo" topics. There are no "elephants in the living room" that everyone avoids discussing. A well-coached family has developed the communication

As parents, we often discover we are unable to coach our own family members.

skills to talk about anything.

- The family can communicate with ease and skill and take well-thought-out action, even on topics with emotional content.

- There is a high degree of trust and personal care among/between family members.

- There are open discussions and commitments by all family members regarding promises, requests, and reliability.

- There is no "pretending" on the level-of-competence scale. Everyone is comfortable acknowledging when they are a beginner.

- When breakdowns do occur, discussion instead of argument can take place. Family members can hear mature dialogue and they can respond rather than react.

- There is minimal gossip within the family. Most conversations, including feedback, are considerate and openly shared, and cordial hypocrisy has been eliminated.

- They all understand the tools that are available and practice the skills of communication. They fully appreciated the impact of a promise and how quickly trust can be betrayed by a broken promise.

- They have a clear mission/purpose for their family wealth, and every family member can state it accurately. This mission is based on the agreed common values the family has identified as a team.

- Family members are active in the family philanthropies, and philanthropy is an integral part of their planning strategy.

- Family members have a long-range vision of where

they fit in the family mission. They know what is expected of them to qualify for any role they choose, as well as the meaning of managing their commitments.

- Adult children are given the authority to be responsible for their own lives and families. They discover how to be part of the larger collective of the family and still be respected and valued individuals.

- Well-coached family members exhibit a remarkable lack of fear and a sense of self-assurance without arrogance or pride, and they believe that, as a family team, they can deal with any issue that may confront them.

- They appreciate their strength as a family. Instead of seeing a family of beneficiaries as a burden, they see it as an opportunity to build together.

- They look to their family as a team and believe that the family itself rather than money is the true wealth.

The above are all healthy signs of a well-coached and well-prepared family and can be used as "reference questions" to provide a family with a baseline from which to evaluate a prospective coach. Most importantly, they are signs that the next generation are learning (or have learned) how to identify issues, resolve them in a family-friendly manner, and are realists about the levels of competence required to be good stewards of the family's wealth.

Chapter 6 Summary

Life is constantly changing. We can fight change, feel uncomfortable, and try to avoid it or we can embrace it. Succession and wealth transfer is a major change. Family members' lack of preparation is the single largest risk to transitioning an estate. Often, this lack of preparation is a result of the resistance to change and fear of giving up control.

Next steps of family preparedness, after learning trust and communication skills, identifying family values and developing a family wealth mission/purpose statement, is for the estate planning team to review the estate plans and compare them with the family wealth mission/to identify conflicts. From this process, the role-development coach and family members identify the needs and roles to fulfill the estate plans and family wealth mission/purpose. The qualifications and performance standards/conditions of satisfaction for these roles are developed.

This phase in preparation of the family for succession requires a third party—an objective and experienced family coach with excellent references from families they have worked with. This chapter specified the characteristics to look for in a coach and the characteristics of a well-coached family.

CHAPTER

7

The Fourth Step: Preparing Your Family Members

"The two most important days in your life are the day you are born and the day you find out why."

—unknown author

Succeeding in preserving and growing wealth intergenerationally requires future generations to be proactively prepared to be good stewards of the family wealth and values. It is a long-term process that, while ideally begun early, it's never too late to start. It is the best investment a family will ever make.

Some common tracks for family members' preparedness for succession:

- Experience in the family business, or experience managing the family investments/assets and or/real estate.

- Experience in a nonfamily business.

- Experience through involvement in family philanthropy.

- Experience through involvement in philanthropic endeavors outside the family.

- Education and/or training.

- All the above, or a combination of some of the above.

Let's look at the first three of these in detail.

Experience in the Family Business

Family leaders may have a well-thought-out list of roles they perceive need to be filled, and each leader approaches this in whichever way he or she thinks will work. At various points in time, roles are offered to whomever the leaders believe can fulfill the role successfully, or they start them at the bottom to work their way up. They may mentor them directly or provide a mentor.

Family members' perceptions of actual roles required may be entirely different from one another. Younger people might strive to feel more independent and may be less willing to accept responsibility for things outside their individual focus. When family members experience a strong model of parental leadership, they may think they need only one person to head up family asset management or the family business. Family members begin to (consciously or unconsciously) defer their involvement to someone else, perhaps an older or more involved sibling, another family member, or even an advisor.

The conversations necessary to define roles are rarely held with the input of the entire family, and usually without considering the family wealth mission. More often than not, families do not have a family wealth mission to begin with. Also, the concept of qualification and performance standards required by these roles is not in the regular purview of the professional advisor's training or the family's. Therefore, it is vaguely assumed that they will be addressed over time by osmosis, family members, executors, or trustees. Somehow, some way, the perception is that age, college education, and living will prepare the family members to become good stewards and role takers.

Sometimes family members get "vacuumed into" the business and swept up in daily business responsibilities based on perceived experience and/or skills. Expectations get set, and life moves inexorably down a road without in-depth conversations. Presumptive foundations are laid, and expectations built on those foundations, and the expectations often prove to be grossly incorrect. Family members begin to feel like square pegs being forced into round holes. When this happens in any family, rebellion can occur, discontent can set in, or a family can operate in cordial hypocrisy.

Our research has revealed that a significant percentage of family members have various reasons to choose not to take a working position within the family; they may have no desire to be involved in the management of assets. College education may take place far from home, opening the world's borders, establishing new peer relationships, and bringing huge changes in the information and opportunities open to family members. Perhaps a family member falls in love with someone from another country. In these instances, an identity begins to form totally separate from the family. All their life experiences tend to offer family members alternatives their parents never had and may result in a choice to not work within the family business or to not manage the family assets.

Experience in a Nonfamily Business

Some leaders of families require family members to gain experience in a similar type of family business, or the family member chooses on his or her own to do this. At a later point, they may join the family business. The premise is that the family member will learn best practices of another company and bring them back to the family business. Also, the family member will more readily be treated as an employee, as opposed to having to work through the automatic label of "entitled family member."

Experience Through Involvement in Family Philanthropy

Our research on ninety-one family foundations[14] indicated some remarkable differences in the attitudes of family members, depending on whether they were involved early in the family philanthropy or not. Our research also revealed many missed opportunities for family members to be involved in family philanthropy. These opportunities are often unifying and personally fulfilling for family members and are opportunities to learn and test family values. Here are the differences our research revealed:

Differences in Attitudes Related to Involvement in Family Philanthropy

Next generation involved in family philanthropy	"If the family loses its wealth, we can earn it back."	Values determine who they are.
Next generation not involved in family philanthropy	"Avoid risks for fear of losing the family wealth because once it's lost, it's gone forever."	They have a sense that money and material possessions determine who they are.

An orthopedic surgeon we know has spent his annual vacation for the last thirty years taking 20 – 34 doctors and nurses and two to three young adults to various remote areas in Central and South America to spend a few weeks helping indigenous people who lack medical care. He provides a portable operating room, medical services, and medical supplies. The young adults help wherever and however needed. They sleep in huts, get to know the local families, and work long, hard hours.

---

14. Roy O. Williams and Professor Newman Peery of UOP Eberhardt School of Business, private research titled "Early Training, Family Foundations, and Philanthropic Activity," November 2, 2001.

As a result of this experience, many of the young adults later become doctors or similar professionals and continue volunteering to provide services to those in need. They understand the value of helping others and that money or material possessions do not determine who they are. They realized that their values, hard work, ingenuity, and problem-solving capacity are part of who they are and that they will always have these qualities and skills. They know they can take care of themselves and others, and that they can survive.

The factors behind this surprising difference in attitudes are complex. One of the lessons here is to provide children opportunities to express their values and to explore their values along with the family values. This is part of preparing family members to become good stewards, develop their own sense of self-esteem, and let money be a tool and a storehouse for the family endeavors instead of a definition of who they are.

A study conducted by Fidelity Charitable, which has grown to become one of the most influential charities in the world, found that philanthropic giving is increasingly a family affair, inclusive of the young children in the family.

Being involved with philanthropy at an early age educates children in many of the skills required in almost every walk of life. Children embrace philanthropy, unaware of all the skills they are learning. They are natural philanthropists because they have big hearts and more energy, time, and focus than many adults. They do not see the barriers and challenges adults perceive, so they are unhindered by cynicism. With a little direction and support, they discover what is meaningful to them, view problems as chal-

Being involved with philanthropy at an early age educates children in many of the skills required in almost every walk of life. Children embrace philanthropy, unaware of all the skills they are learning.

lenges, and come up with solutions. Helping those in need bene-fits the helper as much as, and often more than, the recipients.

A thirteen-year-old granddaughter commented to her grandfather that she had read the Family Wealth Mission Statement, and the specific actions the family was taking and gift they were making to a charity was inconsistent with the Family Wealth Mission Statement. Granddad discussed it with her and declared, "Because you took the time to read, learn, and explain the incongruence, I agree with you, and we will not take the action we planned." The grandfather said his granddaughter grew right in front of him.

"I was trained from the beginning to work, to save, and to give."
—John Rockefeller Jr.

Evidence shows that children who participate actively in philanthropy benefit in the following ways:

- They have increased well-being, are happier and more successful, and achieve more academically.

- They learn about worlds beyond their own experience, and they learn how to appreciate the insights and perspectives of others.

- They learn communication skills, develop confidence in public speaking, and learn how to make a case and how to organize.

- They learn how to choose a charity, which requires research, fund-raising, and entrepreneurial skills.

- They learn tolerance and empathy, as well as decision-making, conflict-resolution, leadership, and social skills and behaviors.

- They gain intrapersonal and interpersonal understanding while working collaboratively and constructively in groups, and they learn how to take the lead.

- They learn how to become change-makers and about the multiplier effect of small acts, as well as the larger impact those small acts can have on communities.

The top four concerns affluent parents have for their children can be addressed proactively through parents being actively involved in philanthropy and providing children the opportunity, from an early age, to participate with them:[15]

- Too much emphasis on material things: **60 percent**

- Naive about the value of money: **55 percent**

- Spend beyond their means: **52 percent**

- Have their initiative ruined by affluence: **50 percent**

> *"Too often, a vast collection of possessions ends up possessing its owner."*
> **—Warren Buffett**

At some point in time, many successful families find that solely building and preserving wealth becomes an unsatisfying goal by itself, and it does not necessarily reflect their personal, long-term hopes for their children. At this juncture, the heads of families may choose to focus on wealth being a launching pad for good and a vehicle to create opportunities for family members, as opposed to being a "threat or burden" to them. Also, many affluent families wish to leave a legacy of social good.

Philanthropy provides the next generation with a powerful opportunity to develop character, caring, and life skills through interacting with advisors, mentors, and real-time challenging scenarios while contributing to society.

The family's values and mission are inculcated, providing the compass and bedrock foundation for thinking and action. Philanthropy provides more occasions for families to converse, collaborate, and form a team to help others while solidifying the

---

15. US Trust Survey of Affluent Americans XIX, December 2000.

individual families inside the larger family. It can break the cycle of selfishness that permeates cultures today and the disconnection and dissociation described as "affluenza." Successful family leaders are active in philanthropy, and it forms an integral part of their planning strategy.

Through the process of identifying the family values and the family wealth mission/purpose statement, the family often recognizes how a family foundation could support those values. Consequently, some heads of families decide to create a family foundation. This is an excellent vehicle to create a family legacy and support good causes while providing an unparalleled opportunity for learning. Although there are tax benefits that come with this type of charitable giving, family foundations may be subject to greater IRS scrutiny. Having a family foundation provides more flexibility in which causes can be supported because the foundation controls those decisions. How-

Successful family leaders are active in philanthropy, and it forms an integral part of their planning strategy.

ever, private foundations cost more to operate than donor-advised funds, have less generous treatment of tax deductions for donations (30 percent for cash/20 percent for property) and must make gifts of at least 5 percent of the assets each year. Given that tax laws and government regulations change frequently, you are advised to use your tax and legal advisors to assist in making financial decisions.

Needs and Roles

In addition to the family business, having a private foundation provides a variety of additional needs and roles for family members. It often meets the interests of family members who have little, if any, interest in business or in managing wealth. The process of comparing the estate plans with the family wealth mission/purpose, identifying the needs to be met and the roles required to meet those needs, and opening role choice to all family members reveals to both the family leaders and the family members each family member's unique "giftedness," interests, and motivation.

The dominant aptitudes and interests in each family member are discovered, sometimes for the first time, and the family members can be provided with opportunities to carry forward a portion of the family mission. In some instances, their interests may result in following a career track outside the family business. Successful families work hard at accurately matching up family member's skills, interests, and competencies with mission, needs, and roles to maximize their growth. This proves effective for the entire family and the estate.

During this process, family leaders have the opportunity to make each family member aware that the family is committed to them realizing their fullest self-potential, whatever that may be. The portrait painter might play a role in overseeing a family philanthropy devoted to supporting the arts. In that role, he

The focus on values allows the belief system of the individual and the family to lead, as opposed to the wealth leading.

or she could evaluate the impact of the family's philanthropy dollars, discover better uses for the philanthropy dollars, and discuss new opportunities. Role options in philanthropy can draw in and offer more opportunities for family members who do not appear to fit into the family unit.

Measuring Readiness for Responsibility and Accountability

Family leaders often ask, "How do I measure the level of readiness of my family members for responsibility and accountability?" And this is the proverbial follow-up question: "How much do I give them, and when?" The readiness level of family members to manage wealth responsibly correlates with the overall readiness of family leaders to prepare the family proactively for the transition of their wealth and values. The focus on values allows the belief system of the individual and the family to lead, as opposed to the wealth leading the conversation. Family members being unprepared to be accountable and responsible is weighted 25 percent of the failure rate of wealth transfers and succession.

In chapter 3, we provided a 10-Question Quiz to use in assessing your wealth transition plan. Below is a second quiz for parents to use in measuring family members' readiness for responsibility and accountability for wealth transfer. To how many of the following questions can you answer "Yes"?

After the quiz, we will examine each of these ten questions in detail and review their relationship to a successful transition of wealth.

Checklist for Parents to Measure Family Members' Readiness		
	Question	Yes or No
1.	Have you included the entire family, including spouses and children over the age of sixteen, in the development of your family wealth mission/purpose statement?	
2.	Are you prepared to model inclusive communication strategies, encourage the input of family members, and make appropriate modifications to support a codesigned estate plan?	
3.	Have you created a family culture that encourages family members to participate in management of the family assets?	
4.	Are you comfortable sharing the estate plans and documents with your family before you pass?	
5.	Have your family and estate planners compared the estate plans with the family wealth mission for alignment, and have conflicts been resolved?	

6.	Has your family developed specific, observable, and measurable qualification and performance standards for determining family members' readiness to receive wealth?	
7.	Have family members codesigned the incentives and opportunities made possible as a result of the wealth?	
8.	Does your family provide opportunities and incentives for the younger children to participate in philanthropic grant-making decisions?	
9.	Have conflicts among family members been amicably resolved, and do your family members have the skills to resolve future conflicts?	
10.	Is the program of preparation under way, with agreed-upon alternatives for each eligible family member in the event that his or her preparation time table or completeness for a role is unmet?	
	Total number of "yes" answers	

These questions are sufficient to gauge the progress of the preparation level within most wealth transfer situations. Fully prepared family leaders will have "Yes" answers to all ten check-points, greatly reducing the risk of failure in transitioning wealth and values to the family members. (Recall that 70 percent of wealth transitions fail.[16]) Again, the factors that are critical to the 30 percent who do succeed are; role preparation of family members, learned skills, and practiced behavior of communication and trust within the family, agreed-upon family values, a family wealth mission/purpose statement, alignment of the estate plans with the family wealth mission/purpose, identification of needs and roles, and qualifications and performance standards.

---

16. Richard Beckhard and W. Gibb Dyer, "Managing Continuity in the Family-Owned Business," Organizational Dynamics, Summer 1983, AMA, p.5.

The steps on this survey are listed in sequential form, and you can use them as a year-to-year measure of progress.

Now we will examine each of these ten questions in detail and review their relationship to a successful transition of wealth.

Question 1. Have you included the entire family, including spouses and children over the age of sixteen, in the development of your family wealth mission/purpose statement?

In chapter 3, we discussed the importance of families having a Family Wealth Mission Statement. Now we want to discuss the importance of including spouses and teenagers over the age of sixteen in the development of a Family Wealth Mission Statement. The strategy for achieving the family wealth mission, and the communication required to navigate it, is an intrinsic part of forming a family team. It sets the foundation for what the family will require to achieve the family mission.

This process provides the opportunity for the following generation to be influenced by both parents and to develop a shared commitment to the same values, family wealth mission, and strategy. Including spouses in this process communicates a powerful and clear message. They have direct influence over the next generation, and their buy-in and support of the mission statement are essential. Our experience has consistently shown us that families generate a unifying solidarity behind the agreed-on family wealth mission.

Question 2. Are you prepared to model inclusive communication strategies, encourage the input of family members, and make appropriate modifications to support a codesigned estate plan?

A strong foundation of communication skills that build trust and relationship is essential within the family team. Without this fundamental skill to coordinate effective action in the family, manage moods, and build trust, all other activities are at the risk of failure. To succeed, each family member must commit to learning healthy communication practices to deepen trust within the family. *It is by learning to talk about the distrust that the family can build trust.*

Through communication, the mission statement becomes "actionable." For example, when a family states that education is important to them in their mission statement, an estimate of the financial assets required to support the educational concerns of the family is placed in an education account. If "enjoying our rewards" is identified in the mission statement as a family value, a budget, destinations, timing, and a person to spearhead the events are identified.

Although there will be disagreement (sometimes strident) early on in discussions, the ability of all voices to get "their two cents in" becomes an important interaction to demonstrate that everyone in the family is valuable, important, and worth hearing. Along with listening come learning and understanding. As the poet David Whyte says, "No one has to change, but everyone has to have the conversation."

Our experience has consistently shown us that families generate a unifying solidarity behind the agreed-on family wealth mission.

Question 3. Have you created a family culture that encourages family members to participate in the management of the family assets?

Fulfilling the family wealth mission/purpose requires family members' willingness to make sacrifices (in terms of time and income) to achieve the family wealth mission/purpose objectives. This process encourages family members to identify specific actions and behaviors required to manage the family assets.

Roles are created based on the strategy required to fulfill the family wealth mission. They are often constrained by structure (e.g., limited partner versus general partner, or foundation trustee versus investment trustee, corporate executive, money manager, investment advisor liaison, real property manager).

Depending on the structure to be served, those needs and roles may range from Chief Financial Officer to Director of the Family Foundation to Family Office Executive. The role may be as specific as "Manager of Investment Fund Advisors" or as broad as "Advisor." The needs and roles can be active (president of the family company) or inactive (passive recipient of wealth distributions.)

Proactively addressing the family's questions and concerns provides an opportunity to produce clarity and understanding without the added emotional upheaval resulting from the loss of a family member.

A strictly wealth (assets) management organization has a substantially different set of needs and roles to be filled than a family who manages a family enterprise (business), plus a foundation, plus a series of trusts, plus a pool of assets, plus a family council. The definition of these roles must be developed with the entire family's involvement, and where necessary, the participation of expert advisors.

Question 4. Are you comfortable sharing the estate plans and documents with the family before you pass?

Our research indicates that it is always preferable to surface objections or concerns *before* wealth is transferred than to have those differing views emerge later, risking disputes and lawsuits. The listening process itself, properly coached, builds communication skills and trust. Surfacing the questions and concerns sooner rather than later creates an opportunity to produce clarity and understanding without the added pressure of emotional upheaval. It incorporates the general notion of seeking first to understand (the others) and then to be understood (as an individual). This models effective behavior the family members can reasonably expect from siblings and their spouses. A final consensus on strategic direction can be reached sooner with the assistance of a competent family coach. Having these conversations as a family allows everyone to hear the important conversations at the same time.

Often, family leaders avoid sharing their estate plans with family members because of the concern that this knowledge could become a disincentive or otherwise negatively impact the family. Our experience has shown that the opposite occurs when family leaders decide to share the estate plans with the family at this point in the process. The family has learned trust and communication skills; identified their family values; developed their family wealth mission; identified and developed the needs, roles, qualification and performance standards for these roles and for advisors; and family members have chosen the roles they want to fill. They are the family team.

Question 5. Have the family and estate planners compared the estate plans with the family wealth mission for alignment, and have conflicts been resolved?

The family, coaches, and advisors have identified and resolved the inevitable conflicts that exist between the estate planning documents developed by the estate planning team and the family values and family wealth mission/purpose developed by the entire family. The comparison of these two documents may yield more roles and responsibilities to be addressed.

This is not the moment to assign family members to one role or another. It is the time to identify the roles themselves, perhaps to be combined or further subdivided later. The required competencies and experience first need to be developed.

Question 6. Has your family developed specific, observable, and measurable performance standards for determining family members' readiness to receive wealth?

Distributing wealth based on a family member's age as opposed to his or her readiness is a recipe for trouble. We recommend that the family discuss the standards and qualifications for receiving wealth. For example, a matriarch might distribute funds only when her son holds a full-time position. The question for each family member is, "What are fair requirements for you to receive wealth in a way that will allow you to thrive?" This can be a way to enter the conversation with the entire family.

Failure to meet the qualification may require another family member take on the role for an interim period or outside (nonfamilial) assistance from an industry professional who is held to the same standards of performance. A family board or a trustee may then step in to manage the wealth until the family member is able to demonstrate that he or she is meeting the required standards. Developing the required qualifications is a learning process, similar to learning new skills for communicating with each other, building trust, and navigating successful wealth transfer.

Stuart and Hubert Dryfus first introduced a five-stage model for assessing levels of adult skill acquisition in 1986.[17] The stages included Novice, Advanced Beginner, Competence, Proficiency, and Expertise. This is a significant contribution to the field of learning and education because it establishes a way for people to determine when they have learned something at the level of being able to take new action as opposed to simply understanding. For example, to say you can drive a car may mean you are able to read signs, press the right pedal, and use the appropriate turn signal. Being able to adjust the vehicle's speed on a turn in wet conditions requires a higher level of skill, taking into consideration mechanics of understanding, along with the situation in which they exist.

In our work with families, we have observed that individuals move through eight levels of learning in the domain of family wealth transfer. Being able to identify where you find you are on the scale, along with the standard of skill expected at that level, enables you to shift what may be a frustrating mood to one of ambition. For example, if I am frustrated because I don't understand the underpinnings of my trust, I can look at these stages and declare myself a pre-beginner based on the standards established

---

17. Mind Over Machine: The Power of Human Intuition and Expertise in the Era of the Computer, chapter 1 (New York: The Free Press) 1986), 50.

(and acknowledged by the rest of the family). Once I see there is much that I don't know that I don't know, I can take some of the pressure off myself and begin the process of becoming a beginner.

To declare myself a beginner, I now have a different mood as it relates to the complex and important domain of wealth transfer. In the Western culture, and in some competitive families, the idea of being a beginner, making mistakes, and failing to "already know" is a sign of weakness. Locating yourself within these eight levels of learning is a useful way to take responsibility for your learning and enjoy the journey of gaining competence to manage wealth successfully.

These may also be useful standards to consider when a family member is ready to move into a new role in the family business, council, or board position. We provide examples below of how the levels are relevant specifically in a family council or philanthropy.

The Williams Group's eight levels of learning are as follows:

1. **Self-Declared Ignorance—I do not wish to learn that particular subject; it does not interest me. I comfortably declare my igno- rance in that domain.** This may manifest as an overall decline to get involved in anything related to the family wealth, a family council, or philan- thropy. In this case, building skill in assessing the competence of advisors would be useful.

2. **Pretender—I am going to pretend. I will find a way to look good and blame negative results on someone or something else.** This may show up when someone is obliged to take a seat on the family council without being prepared for the position. The person who donates blindly to charitable causes and then discovers the orga- nization is not legitimate would fall into this cat- egory. Family members who are expected to take

positions in the company they don't want may end up pretending to know what they are doing in an attempt to save face.

3. **Pre-Beginner—I am unaware of what I don't know that I don't know.** In this case, the individual is unaware of the existence of a family council or philanthropic avenues. They may actually exist in the family, just not in the reality of that family member. In a more common example, a family member does not know the importance of understanding how power of attorney works or what the parents' wishes are.

4. **Beginner—I want to learn. I declare myself a learner and will begin to learn and open myself to discovery. I am willing to make mistakes. I am open to being coached.** A member of the next generation may make a request to learn more about how he or she can become a member on the family council and agree to take the steps to meet the standard for participating. The family member may decide to learn how a charitable organization applies the funds it receives and hold them accountable to producing a yearly review of what impact they had.

5. **Minimally Competent—I can accomplish the tasks in front of me with minimal direction. I follow the plan and do not stray from it.** For example, you can follow the mandate of your role on the family council and/or contribute to the same charities.

6. **Competent—I am able to manage all the aspects of my role, including planning. I have**

a sense of the bigger picture and the action necessary to achieve the goal. At this level, you may be able to develop a plan for improving communication and effectiveness for the family council. You may be able to identify a plan for aligning family giving to charitable organizations for greater impact.

7. **Virtuoso—I am able to prioritize, see patterns that require adjustment, and understand the bigger picture of what we want to achieve.** At this level, you may be able to see the breakdowns in how the family council currently operates and make recommendations for streamlining communication, identify what needs to be communicated, and ensure ongoing success. You may see the historical performance of the long-time recipient of family giving, compare it to current events, and make recommendations to go in a new direction.

8. **Master—My gut instinct leads my actions. I set the vision and the guidelines for accomplishing goals.** At this level, decisions are made based on experience, combined with a facility of having a sense of what is right. For example, a recommendation may arise during a family council meeting, and you know if it will serve or disrupt the family. You hold the standards and direction for how family giving will reflect the family's goals and align with the family legacy.

History is replete with stories of the person who began "in the mailroom" or as a "summer employee" and worked his or her way to lead the enterprise. These are examples of the gradual development of various levels of competence and a steady broadening of experience. The question is, "How is the performance of the holder of roles to be measured and evaluated?"

Competence does not come simply from educational credentials. Holding a position for twenty years does not automatically make anyone an expert. It is essential for the family (in participation with its advisors) to develop criteria to measure relevant experience, education, and the performance of the metrics for each role. If saving is a requirement, for example, it may mean the family member works with an accountant to learn to manage their finances.

The guidelines are not etched in stone but represent generally accepted levels of competence that can be clearly understood and measured. This allows the other family members to have a common platform for expressing their satisfaction, or in some cases, dissatisfaction with how a family member is performing in a particular role.

When the need for competency is subverted by expedience and a family member is placed in a role before he or she is fully prepared, special mentoring and/or tutoring accommodations are required.

Question 7. Have family leaders codesigned the incentives and opportunities made possible as a result of the wealth?

When the next generation is clear about the opportunities the wealth can provide, they can consider their own interests and how they may be connected.

Engaging in a dialogue with family members about the incentives required to receive distributions is both empowering and secures buy-in to the behaviors that support the family values. When the next generation is clear about the opportunities the wealth can provide, they can consider their own interests and how they may be connected.

For example, we worked with a family member who was a teacher and was struggling trying to make ends meet for his own growing family. He was subject to the unpredictable educational system that gave the longer-term positions to tenured teachers. He was doing his best to wait out the uncertain time period of when he would be given a full-time position. In a family meeting, the family was discussing the criteria for joining the family office as a family liaison and philanthropy strategist. The role, skills, and qualifications were outlined to include researching skills, aptitude as a strong relationship builder, a collaborative nature, and financial savviness. At once, the siblings all looked to this individual as having the majority of the skills. After agreeing to terms for what it would require to become competent in reading financial statements, a new career was born, and perhaps most importantly, family relationships strengthened.

The Cavanaugh family decided that any family member having a "significant" decision-making financial responsibility role within the family enterprise was required to have at least an undergraduate degree and five years of "progressively responsible experience" working in a corporation not controlled by the family. They defined "significant" as "any role capable of obligating more than 1 percent of the family's liquid assets during a calendar year."

Question 8. Does your family provide opportunities and incentives for your younger children to participate in philanthropic grant-making decisions?

Setting the standard of encouraging younger family members to give happens at the leadership level. Family leaders can demonstrate a commitment to philanthropy by matching contributions, donating to charities their grandchildren care about, or providing incentives for family members who demonstrate they have tracked the impact of their giving and can show how their values live in their actions. Inviting members of various charity or philanthropic organizations to demonstrate the impact their organizations have had at a family meeting or distributing activities of young philanthropists may be a way to expand the scope of possibilities for younger children. Earlier in this chapter, we discussed the benefits of philanthropy for family members.

"How wonderful that no one need wait a single moment to improve the world."
—Anne Frank

Question 9. Have conflicts among family members been amicably resolved, and do your family members have the skills to resolve future conflicts?

Teaching family members to resolve their own conflicts enables them to move through a current issue, *and* it provides them with the skills to navigate the inevitable and unknowable challenges they will face as a family unit. Establishing levels of learning as a path to competence takes the pressure off of having to "get it right" immediately. To know everyone is learning to communicate with new tools together creates a mood of tolerance and support for each other and invites new ways of engaging that were perhaps not possible before. Having the confidence that they can work through adversity together is a vital part of family harmony. When new, productive communication skills have been woven into the fabric of everyday interactions, the following generations will inherit the same set of valuable tools for collaboration and trust.

Teaching family members to resolve their own conflicts enables them to move through a current issue while providing them with the skills to navigate the inevitable and unknowable challenges they will face as a family unit.

Question 10. Is the program of preparation under way, with agreed-upon alternatives for each eligible family member in the event that his or her preparation time table or completeness for a role is unmet?

It is vital for the preparation to transfer wealth to happen proactively, as opposed to waiting for the moment it must transfer. Playing the game "while the game is going on" enables the heirs to become competent in learning how to manage wealth, applying new communication skills, building relationships, being mentored where necessary, and reevaluating the role(s) they have been given.

In some cases, that may mean changing their career trajectory from being a company successor to starting their own business, changing the terms of their beneficiary status, or proving they can save money. In one of our client families, the father was unwilling to provide his daughter with a regular distribution until she could demonstrate that she saved a certain amount of money. After working with a personal financial accountant, the daughter exceeded expectations, including her own. She discovered that not only could she save, but the increase in her self-esteem enabled her to begin to consider new business ventures for herself.

Billy was asked to vote on decisions involving complex, long-term commercial property exchanges simply because he owned the same percentage of the family estate as the other brothers and sisters. Billy was doing a terrific job as a specialty interior designer and loved his work. Although he had no interest in real estate, he did have a vested interest in the family making good real estate decisions.

He felt pressured, inadequate, and unable to do the analysis needed to vote intelligently on important issues involving real estate. He finally told the family that he was "unqualified" to make those types of decisions and that he had no intention of reshaping his life to get the education and experience required to become competent. He then asked his younger sister (who had a master's degree in real estate finance and was the financial VP of the family corporation) to advise him on how he should vote. She was comforted by his candor, accepted the added responsibility (which made her even more careful in her analysis), and effectively doubled her voting power in the family enterprise. Everyone felt better, decisions were made more quickly, and harmony ensued.

Be concerned about any family member who accepts any responsibility thrust on her or him. A healthier response would be for the family member to engage the family leadership in a "Why me?" conversation. Healthier yet is the family who understands the skills and interests of each family member and communicates their encouragement and continued support.

It is important to take steps to confirm basic interests, assess skills and competencies, and discuss willingness to obtain additional training and experience for the role being considered. What the family should seek is a good match. If a family member is only "able to perform at a minimally competent skill level," that is insufficient. Much more learning may be required to move to a proficient level. This process serves the family unit and the family members.

What families seek is the sincere expression of interest in a role. A *sincere* expression of interest means that a family member:

- Completely understands the role, the qualifications required, and the standards for performing the role competently.

- Has an appreciation and affinity for the role.

- Is likely to find personal fulfillment and happiness in preparing for the role, addressing the family's needs, and filling the role.

What happens when more than one person wants to be the future CEO of the family enterprise? What happens when two family members want to be Vice President for Marketing? How do issues get resolved if there is a conflict?

What families seek is the sincere expression of interest in a role.

Family leaders must take care here to avoid "shutting down" or prematurely selecting one family member at the price of alienating or losing the involvement of the other family members.

If the discussion can be well grounded by using the well-thought-out, observable, measurable qualifying standards and levels of competence the family developed, then the rival siblings will usually reach the same conclusion about who is most qualified and has an affinity for the role. The important thing is to have the conversation. *Our research shows that the best way to begin the dialogue is to start it based on the qualifying standards.* A focus on the standards removes the blame, judgment, and personalization of the issue at hand.

With the notion of "family teamwork" established, with agreement on the family's wealth mission, and learned skills of communication, a solid foundation exists to help resolve challenging conflicts.

In instances where there are highly charged discussions about seemingly intractable conflicts revolving around asset management roles, family leaders can explore the two themes of "careful analysis" and "open discussion" with skilled coaching to resolve the issue successfully. It is far wiser to confront these challenges proactively with appropriate support than after the fact with legal counsel.

An openly competing set of wishes declared by family members is much healthier for the family than concealed competitive behavior. Out of a fear of conflict, family leaders may avoid this discussion. The problem of competing for a future role is much more manageable than concealed competition or fear and loathing about being involved in the management and responsibility of the family wealth.

Of all the problems that family leaders face, sorting out which family member is destined for which role benefits most from skilled coaching. It is valuable to reframe issues such as "It was Dad's decision" or, "I knew Mom was going to side with you; she always does!" in an atmosphere of *"What's best for the family and for you?"* That reframing has shown to be most effective when done with an outside family-coaching professional. As most parents learn, they are often not the best coaches for a family member.

The Martell family built a $200 million company. Their sons were educated at Ivy League universities, and both excelled in business. Competitively encouraged, the sons were always trying to out-perform one another. This competitive behavior carried through to auto purchases, home building, and managing sectors of the family company. Due to the conflicts this caused, the parents hired consultants to mediate between the brothers. The behavior was becoming destructive to the family company, threatening its financial stability, and severely hurting their relationship as a family.

A competent family coach was brought in, interviewed the family members and their spouses, and began a series of family meetings. The family realized that the behaviors originated with parental encouragement of competitive behavior. The family learned new skills of collaborative team building and communication and rebuilt trust. As a result, the sons found much pleasure and connection in collaborating and ceased competing in a destructive manner.

Family members need to participate actively in the process of resolving their competition for a future role. The resolution emerges from a closer examination of their motivation, interest levels, competencies, and time required for full preparation for their role.

The coach will initiate in-depth conversations with family members, involve them in three-way discussions about the role and its requirements, and other available roles that might benefit from their skills. This process requires a commitment to monthly meetings with the competing family members and the coach. A coaching plan is established to support the family member who will pursue a new direction or role.

Family wealth disputes get resolved for the greater good of the family.

Once the issue has been resolved, the family members share their "findings" (the suggested resolution) to the entire family at a family meeting. In making that announcement personally, together, they model the behaviors for how conflict within the family is resolved, reinforce the understanding that they are part of a family team, *and demonstrate that family-wealth disputes get resolved for the greater good of the family.*

When properly handled, this is simply another bump in the road that presents an effective opportunity to learn, teach, and strengthen the family.

Preparing family members for future roles cannot be a general notion; it must deal with specifics. If education preparation is required, the questions need to focus on the required educational degree and time frame. If preparation deals with alternative learning, where should it come from, and how will it be measured? Is formal licensure or admittance to the profession required? Is there a requirement for maintaining licensure or certification for the role to be taken in the family wealth management? And who covers the bill for further education or classes for professional certification exams? If the goal is to prepare for a family responsibility role, then the family should foot the bill. Perhaps the payment for further education or training (including a living allowance until completion) is "forgiven" at a rate of 20 percent per year of employment within the family enterprise.

Professional advisors are aware of numerous options to handle these situations, and agreement on the program for role preparation is ultimately the family's. Families who transition successfully do not expect the financial managers, accountants, or lawyers to decide on a development program for family members because this type of conflict is not a legal, tax, or financial one. It is a family communication and commitment discussion, after which the legal and tax advisors are notified. They provide the structure required to implement what the family wants.

These specifics of development should be detailed and formalized in a "contract" between the family leaders and the family members involved. The contract needs to include the measurement requirements, what further steps will be required if goals are unmet, and what levels of experience (demonstrating growth in operating skill) are needed. For example, maybe the required level of experience is five years of steadily advancing responsibility as an investment advisor with earnings (plus incentives), increasing by no less than 10 percent each year.

Is the experience to be gained in a corporate environment, in an industry similar to that of the family business, or experience abroad? Or is it experience in a functional department such as sales or finance? It is important that changes to the contract/agreement occur only when both parties consent to them.

Changes might be required after a death in the family, the sale of a division, a change in the market, or circumstances surrounding the family enterprise. Make changes to the program of preparation only after thoughtful consideration and acceptance by the all parties involved.

Tom Gannon spoke privately with the family coach. Tom confessed that he was "afraid" for the first time in his life. When the coach asked why, Tom said, "My dad is eighty years old, and he just told me that I am taking over as president of our billion-dollar family business in January. I've worked for Dad all my life, and he's never allowed me to fail. I don't know if it is because he would have been embarrassed or because he wanted to protect me, or both. Now, for the first time in my life, I will not have a safety net, I am going to be allowed to fail…big time…and I'm terrified!" For Tom, the issue was not about being competent to be the president; it was about having the confidence to do so.

What Tom was missing in his life is what Michael Jordan had experienced–failing and going on. Jordan once said, "I've missed more than nine thousand shots in my career. I've lost almost three hundred games. Twenty-six times, I've been trusted to take the game winning shot and missed. I've failed over and over and over again in my life. And that is why I succeed."

It is clearly more meaningful to allow next-generation family members to learn by experiencing normal, small failures than to "protect" them over time, suddenly saddling them with the major and unrelenting responsibility of leadership. While well intended, it is a disservice to protect family members from failing. It conceals weakness. It reduces learning. It fails to teach them how to deal with risk and failure. It artificially creates perfection as the measure. These are serious mistakes, done in the name of love for the children. Take the training wheels off their bikes early, not at age twenty or fifty.

It is important to get a program of preparation under way if it is not already in effect. Courses, specialty instruction, job shadowing, tutoring, and other resources can get the formal preparation jump-started while the conversations are fresh and the passion is still high. Reinforce the elements of the "contract" for family members' preparation by initiating action and announcing that the process is under way, and do it as soon as possible. The family should be prepared to support such preparation financially, whether in the form of tuition, fees, or study. It is, in fact, preparation for the benefit of the entire family.

It is helpful to remember that in most instances parents are not usually good coaches for their own children.

A challenge may arise with a family member who slacks off in his or her efforts to prepare for a role. Perhaps they stop attending classes, fail to show up for mentoring sessions, or begin to miss meetings. What happens then? If the derailment is a simple setback, and easily remedied in a short time, the leaders of the family should be generous in understanding, encouraging the family member to get back on course as soon as possible. The slip should not be ignored. Discussion is warranted. It may be a symptom of unreliability. A more serious derailment may require that interim people be hired (from the outside) to fill the role until the family member has met the family standards for preparation requirements. The hiring of this outside person should be based on observable measurable standards. This person may then mentor this family member.

Finally, if a serious setback occurs, and the reasons for the setback signify that the family member is unlikely to resume an agreed-on preparation course, then a recharting of their involvement is required. The change in course may have nothing to do with their competence, reliability, or sincerity—and little to do with clear business issues. A range of circumstances such as the inability of a role to engage their giftedness or a change of life priorities or health issues may come into view. The roles needed within the corporation may change with time and the marketplace.

In some cases, we have seen family members take an adult "time out" and return to school, or travel, or gain some valuable work experience in an unrelated field, and resume their interest in the role and necessary preparation at a later date. This may result in an agreement to delay the placement of the family member into the agreed-on role until some additional requirements are met. Or, this may require the coach be recalled to support the family member in designing a new path, and reset some targets and role readiness plans.

We cannot prepare (contract) for all eventualities and all forces that are likely to tug a family member off course. However, we can hold them accountable for the time table and preparation that was within their control and to which they agreed. Failure to act on a family member's preparation failures will only lead to more failures.

Scoring the 10-Question Checklist for Family Members' Readiness

The "Family Members' Readiness Self-Checklist" is sequential and can be used as an annual checklist.

The questions are sufficient to gauge the progress of the preparation level of individual family members for wealth transfer. Fully prepared family members will have "Yes" answers to all 10 checkpoints, greatly reducing the risk of failure in transitioning wealth and values.

- Parents able to answer "yes" to seven or more of the ten questions are also closely correlated with those families who have successfully transitioned their wealth. They are most likely to be one of the families out of three who will transition their values and their wealth into a relatively harmonious environment for the benefit of their children and grandchildren. These families are unified in the belief that the unity and harmony of the family is vital for a successful transfer of the financial wealth of the family, and they have taken the necessary steps to ensure this.

- Parents able to answer "yes" to four to six of the ten questions are likely to benefit substantially from efforts to improve the levels of trust and communication within their family. This is fundamental to preparing their family members for wealth and responsibility. In the absence of a substantial effort, however, this group will remain most closely correlated with the 70 percent of the families who fail to transition their wealth effectively. This is the "high return" group that can achieve the largest improvement in their transition odds of success with the least amount of work. As discussed in chapter 4, simply knowing is insufficient; it is critical to take action to offset the risk that family members will be negatively impacted and to take the necessary steps to prevent the family estate's demise.

- Parents able to answer "yes" to three or fewer of the ten questions above are closely correlated to those families who failed to transition their wealth and values successfully. Those families are characterized by a dissipation of wealth among the family members, infighting and hostility within the family, and a loss of family unity in the next generations. It should be clearly understood that those situations can be changed for the better. It requires family leadership and professional coaching assistance to make the changes necessary to increase the odds of a successful transition.

The role preparation of family members, accompanied by learned skills and practiced behavior of communication and trust within the family, agreed-upon family values and family wealth mission/purpose statement, alignment of the estate plans with the family wealth mission/purpose with identification of needs and roles with qualifications and performance standards, are critical to the 30 percent who succeed.

Trust and Communication as They Relate to Family Members' Readiness

The checklist carries with it a presumption that the family works on and maintains a high level of trust and communication within the family, keeps updating and referencing the family wealth mission/ purpose, and closely follows the role readiness course of action. Only with this close attention to preparing family members for wealth with responsibility and accountability can the family move its estate from the "likely to fail" group into the "likely to succeed" group.

The unilateral decision that an eligible family member is not ready for certain information indicates that the family leadership has not prepared that family member for the information. This results in the family member being handicapped in his or her own efforts at self-preparation. For a family member to be "ready" for information on the family's wealth, the parent's income, or the appropriate mission for the family's wealth, the parents' issues and concerns need to be communicated first.

Family members' unpreparedness is a consequence of a breakdown in communication and trust within the family unit. Trust is built when the family leaders say, "I want you to know this information as soon as you have accomplished Task X or Task Y." Family members want, at the very least, to understand what will be required of them, so they need to be in the communication loop. Without this clear understanding mistrust will develop and undermine the eventual transition of the family wealth.

A sudden death within the family leadership, turmoil in the

family or in the personal life of the family members, or changes within the sibling group are other factors that can cause a precipitous change, catching the family members unprepared. Families who already have preparations under way increase the chance of a successful transition even under these unplanned circumstances.

How to Help Family Members Discover Their Optimum Roles in Life

> *"If everyone is thinking alike, then somebody isn't thinking."*
> —**George S. Patton**

Many assessment tools and sources of personal and professional mentoring are available. As family members begin to mature, distinct preferences will evolve. These preferences are not always clearly linked to professional job descriptions. For example, a family member may express an interest in working for the US Coast Guard at age sixteen. You and I may hear, "government job, dangerous, drug smugglers, no chance to build the family wealth, always separated from family." What the young person may be thinking is, "Service to humanity with a rescue organization, working outdoors, association with a tight group of shipmates." There are no thoughts about family, pay, or nearness to siblings.

Family members want, at the very least, to understand what will be required of them, so they need to be in the communication loop.

The following year, the goal may evolve into considering an appointment to the United States Military Academy until the family member finds out that his or her best friend is applying to the University of California at Santa Cruz because "it has a cool program in oceanography!"

In short, expect career assessments to change and evolve over time. Additionally, expect that our "mature" sense of family members' preference may be far from what's in the other family members' minds and far from what is yet to evolve. Successful families use a range of evaluative and test instruments (e.g., questionnaires, interviews) designed to uncover developing preferences of family members.

The most useful family-member interest assessment instruments include family members' preferences for the following:

- Preferred type of activity—physical or mental.

- Preferred work setting and nonwork settings.

- Types of colleagues and learning desired.

- The balance between learning and simply producing.

- The desire to lead or to follow.

- The desire for recognition and personal achievement.

- An objective assessment of current strengths and weaknesses.

- The importance of current peer groups and their decisions.

- The personality type for satisfaction—helping, producing, designing, teaching, etc.

- Potential career paths reflective of preferences consistent with bulleted items above.

Jaime Casap, Google Global Education Evangelist, offers a great way to start the conversation about aspirations and passions. He is credited with saying, "Don't ask kids what they want to be when they grow up; *ask them what problems they want to solve.*" This changes the conversation from "Who do I want to work for?" to *"What do I need to learn to be able to do that?"*

The roles needed within the corporation may change with time and the marketplace. If the family members value the strength of good relationships and are willing to take time out to respond to the needs of those relationships, then that's a good indication that the proper values are in place.

The preparation of family members is a long-term task, beginning with the early establishment of trust and communication, family values, a family wealth mission/purpose statement, individual aspirations, role development, and healthy individual attitudes toward wealth, accountability and responsibility. You will find more about family members self-preparation and accountability in chapter 8. A culture that is predominantly intolerant of mistakes will breed inaction and fear and result in a mood of resignation. Learning as a team allows everyone's input in creating a path forward that they all buy into.

Chapter 7 Summary

This chapter illustrates how everything discussed in previous chapters provides the foundation for preparing family members proactively for successful succession, learning trust and communication skills, identifying family values, discovering individual aspirations, reviewing the estate plans and comparing them with family wealth mission/purpose for congruency, and identifying important key needs and roles with clear performance standards that everyone understands. Cocreating the values, family wealth mission/purpose, and roles is a fundamental ingredient for success. In this chapter, we provided a checklist and discussion on each point for family leaders to use in assessing their readiness and the family members' readiness for responsibility and accountability.

Cocreating the values, family wealth mission/purpose, and roles is a fundamental ingredient for success.

The values of philanthropy in training family members, providing tax reductions, bonding the family unit, teaching family values, and leaving a social legacy were discussed. Also discussed was the value of skilled coaching during the preparation for the succession process. Choosing a professional experienced coach with excellent references from families they have worked with is essential in helping the family navigate contentious issues.

Also discussed were roles and developing a process that involves the entire family to support family members in achieving their full potential and being accountable and responsible. It is important to recognize and accept that world events and personal situations can cause bumps in the road, changes, and disruption. A well-prepared family will be there to help one another learn from and live through those inevitable life "bumps."

Supporting family members to find their optimum role in life, whatever that may be, was covered, and a list of helpful preferences to identify when considering career direction was provided. This chapter also included an in-depth discussion about the fact that issues of trust and communication as they relate to family member readiness for succession can be either high risk or high potential for wealth transfer and succession.

8

The Fifth Step: Family Members' Self-Preparation Responsibilities

"The best day of your life is the one on which you decide your life is your own. No apologies or excuses. No one to lean on, rely on, or blame. The gift is yours—it is an amazing journey—and you alone are responsible for the quality of it. This is the day your life really begins."

—**Bob Moawad**

During the first meeting with the Chanya family, the oldest next-generation family member, Tary, asked, "Why should I get a job? What's the purpose? Grandfather left me ten million dollars in stock, and I'm receiving about nine hundred thousand dollars each year. Like, what's the reason for working? I don't get it."

After several meetings, Tary began to realize that issues of dig-nity, competence, self-reliance, and self-esteem were wrapped up in decisions he needed to make separately from his grandfather's be-quest. He declared himself "a beginner" and set out on a course to pursue a lifelong interest in ecological water quality issues. With the help of a mentor, he identified his interests, prepared himself carefully, worked diligently, and today heads up a successful water company – much to the delight of his parents and family. In another instance, the son-in-law felt his income was insufficient to support the standard of living to which his wife was accustomed, and expect-ed. Further, he felt his work was a poor match for his skills and knew he could be earning a more significant income. In a family meeting, other family members all shared their assessments of his talents and passions. The conversation revealed a new interpretation of what was possible for him, which allowed his father-in-law to support him in new ways. He transitioned to a role that combined his love of the planet and provided him a higher standard of living.

Throughout this book, we have been communicating what suc-cessful families have done to ensure successful transition of their family's values and wealth, with emphasis on the family leaders' re-sponsibilities.

Family leaders frequently asked, "I understand what I need to do, but what responsibilities do the other family members have? It can't all be on our shoulders" and, "What should our family members be doing to prepare themselves for the responsibility of the wealth that has been created?" This chapter responds to these questions and lays out the self-examination family members of successful wealth transition families underwent.

Although our research suggests that parents "accept the input of the family members," this does not mean parents hand over au-thority or control; it does mean sharing information with family members, allowing family members input and influence on major transition decisions, and receiving family members' input with respect and consideration. It also means holding them account-able to their promises and commitments. Millennials today are stepping into very different organizations than the generation before them. They are being asked to participate in companies that are typically much more complex and operating in a more turbulent and fast-moving marketplace. Occasionally we see that the fear of failure is the root of the breakdown of younger family members in taking on more responsibility. They may be saying to themselves, "I'll never be as successful as my parents" or "I'm supposed to know all this by now, so I'd better not ask" or, "Dad has always taken care of this stuff; I have never had to learn."

When a culture of learning is woven into the family, it allows family members to admit what they don't know and ask questions. Learning, as opposed to getting it right the first time, becomes the new norm and establishes a mood of support and curiosity.

To learn is to become competent in a domain. We say a person has learned when he or she can take new action. When assessing competency, or family member readiness, it is helpful to remember the eight levels of competence provided in chapter 7, ranging from beginner to master.

We have distilled the internal processes of successful families into the ten most important checkpoints for individual family members. The list requires honest reflection, and in those instances where the answer is "no", the next question becomes "what conversation is required to make it a "yes".

Occasionally we see that the fear of failure is the root of the break-down of younger family members in taking on more responsibility.

Individual Next-Generation Self-Checklist of Readiness		
	Question	Yes or No?
1.	Are you mentally and emotionally open to participating with your family, learning communication tools, and contributing to develop your family values and family mission statement?	

2.	Do you hold yourself accountable for clearly understanding the difference between knowing (what needs to be done) and doing (what needs to be done), in the best interests of the family unit?	
3.	Do you collaborate in the management of family assets with the entire family, including siblings and spouses?	
4.	Do you understand your present and future role in the estate plans and the mission and purpose of your family wealth?	
5.	Have you actively worked with your family and estate-planning team to understand the estate plans and roles. Do you wish to become prepared?	
6.	Do you understand asset-distribution terms and conditions and support the standards required to receive wealth?	
7.	Have you participated with your family in developing the incentives and opportunities available to you and the standards required for both?	
8.	Have you aligned your personal interests with philanthropic endeavors?	
9.	Does your family support your aspirations?	
10.	Are you taking the necessary steps to become prepared, and are you able to participate fully in family meetings?	
	Total number of "yes" answers	

Question 1. Are you mentally and emotionally open to participating with your family, learning communication tools, and contributing to developing your family values and family mission statement?

Learning communication tools with the family and their professional outside coaches, identifying the family's values, and developing the family mission statement requires taking personal responsibility and giving the process deep thought. It sets the foundation for what will be required for the family to define its wealth mission/purpose. This process helps unite and bond the family toward a legacy of peace and prosperity.

It is one thing to say that you are open to the communication requirements and another to practice communication consistency in real-life situations. The foundation of mutual intrafamily trust is built on the three components of trust: reliability, sincerity, and competence. Trust cannot be sustained without honest, open, and transparent communications. No duplicity. No "spinning." No guile. No manipulation. Just the honest truth, so that the family can take mutual action in a coordinated fashion—action they understand and support, and leads them to accept responsibility for the outcome together. Each role-occupying family member has this responsibility.

It is one thing to say that you are open to the communication requirements and another to practice communication consistency in real-life situations.

Question 2. Do you hold yourself accountable for clearly understanding the difference between knowing (what needs to be done) and doing (what needs to be done), in the best interests of the family unit?

Seldom do failures occur because we didn't *know* what to do. The failures occur because we didn't act in a timely fashion to convert what we *know* into what we *do*. You will be evaluated on how you put what you know into action. Converting knowledge into action can be very challenging, and the fear of failure can result in inaction. Doing what needs to be done requires that you be willing to deal with unavoidable failures, learn how to recover, and move on to the next challenge, armed with an understanding of the causes of the failures and a desire to avoid making the same mistake again. As Buckminster Fuller so eloquently put it, "Mistakes are great; the more I make, the smarter I get."

Question 3. Do you collaborate in the management of family assets with the entire family, including siblings and spouses?

Working with the entire family in managing the family assets requires you commit time and attention to understand the full extent of the family assets, coupled with well-developed communication skills. It is not always easy to speak up and say you don't agree with something the rest of the family is excited about. Resignation and resentment live in the places where we feel we are powerless.

It is in those moments that the window appears for the next generation to have a say in how their future is unfolding. It is no one else's responsibility but your own to speak up and express your point of view on a particular topic. Although it takes courage at times, it is this very authentic and open communication that lies at the core of every high-performing team. Reaching agreement may not always be possible; however, having conversations that provide a platform for each person to be heard creates an opening for alignment. It is not until we feel we have been heard that we can say, "I can live with that."

Question 4. Do you understand your present and future role in the estate plans and the mission and purpose of your family wealth?

Although it takes courage at times, it is this very authentic and open communication that lies at the core of every high-performing team.

In some families, it is just not the norm to ask for help. Or it can actually be frowned upon to ask questions, especially those having to do with the estate. Often it is assumed that the eldest sibling will be the heir to the business or the executor of the estate. Learning what it means to be a shareholder, an owner who does not work in the company, an investor, or even a beneficiary is, in part, uniquely defined by the family itself. The expectations and qualifications for these roles tend to evolve without much conversation.

As time goes by and these roles remain unexamined, it becomes a matter of expectation without ever securing agreement to what is being expected. It is important for you to be honest with yourself and others in considering if you have the level of understanding required to be a responsible steward. It can be daunting to consider the complexities of a foundation, philanthropic responsibilities, and executor responsibilities, let alone the role of communicating with family members outside the business. Asking questions in an attempt to understand the qualifications and performance (conditions of satisfaction) standards that may be formally or informally set for a particular role is the only way to really know what others will expect if the role is accepted.

Question 5. Have you actively worked with your family and estate-planning team to understand the estate plans and roles, and do you wish to become prepared?

Once a role has been chosen, the readiness plan is based on your education, experience, and interests and the family relationship requirements the family has developed for that role. Some roles can be learned by taking a boot-camp version of financial education, having regular conversations with a family advisor with the specific purpose of education, or even shadowing another family member who is currently performing a role you will be moving into, such as sitting on the board or being a liaison to charitable organizations.

There may be a point at which you realize that you can no longer fulfill the requirements of a role you previously agreed to and that others expect from you. Life events, a change in individual focus, or circumstances that change the organi-

The responsibility of managing the commitment to the role for the sake of the family lies with you.

zation itself can contribute to shifting priorities or goals. The responsibility of managing the commitment to the role for the sake of the family lies with you.

Question 6. Do you understand asset-distribution terms and conditions and support the standards required to receive wealth?

A family's distribution policy is typically set by the head of the family, at times driven by estate laws, tax consequences, or the history of how it has always been handled. As a receiving family member, understanding the terms under which you receive assets can be an empowering process. Beneficiaries often struggle with the line between entitlement and expected distribution.

Understanding the terms of why and how the assets are distributed enables you to manage your own financial concerns, plan for your future, and take an active role in meeting the standards identified. For example, if it is the family leader's decision to buy the first home for his or her children, is it expected that they will hold a full-time position to cover the maintenance costs before the title is transferred over? Or if a sibling is to receive regular installments of wealth, is it required that he or she save a certain percentage to continue receiving wealth? Is there a standard set in terms of the amount of the distribution that is allocated for charity or philanthropy?

Open discussions about these expectations and standards that involve the entire family provide an opportunity to gain clarity and alignment. The standards will typically reflect family values, such as saving, giving, employment, or growth percentages.

Question 7. Have you participated with your family in developing the incentives and opportunities available to you and the standards required for both?

The opportunities made possible by significant wealth are exciting, and they can be overwhelming. Being supported in identifying the ways you can make a contribution that resonates with your interests and aspirations is central to your self-confidence and purpose. Family conversations that open new areas of interest, create a supportive environment to share interpretations of other family members' strength, and provide incentives for reaching goals produce a mood of ambition and acceptance.

In one of the families we worked with, a family member had an interest in starting a business. The standard process was to submit a professional business plan and have an outside business advisor review it. As a family, they all reviewed the plan and together made the decision based on specific criteria what amount of money would go toward funding the business. In another example, investment opportunities that pulled from the family wealth beyond a certain dollar amount had to meet criteria related to social responsibility, percentage of profits returned, and opportunities created for other family businesses or members.

Question 8. Have you aligned your personal interests with philanthropic endeavors?

We have seen recurrently that when people donate to organizations for the purpose of tax advantages, they tend to lose interest or miss an opportunity to have a focused and sustained impact on a cause. Often the philanthropic or charitable organizations are determined by the family leader's interests. Teaching younger generations to give based on the values and mission of the family breeds support and interest in the act of giving.

On more than a few occasions, we have seen people who had little direction in their lives find a new way to bring value to their lives and the lives of others through a cause that interests them. If you have formerly felt uncomfortable with wealth, you may find a broader purpose and newfound pride in having an impact in significant ways. Along with demonstrating family values, it can

Teaching younger generations to give based on the values and mission of the family breeds support and interest in the act of giving.

also be a conduit to learning basic financial skills, decision-making skills, and accountability.

Question 9. Does your family support your aspirations?

Diversity in a family can be the source of creativity, acceptance, and sometimes conflict. Not all family members share the same interests or have the same experiences, despite growing up in the same home. The differing ways you live your life can be a source of judgment and cause you to feel ostracized. Conversations that encourage all family members to explore their own interests in a mood of curiosity foster new avenues that may not have been considered before. As successor to the company you may decide you no longer want to run the family business and hopefully your family will support your decision to launch your own career.

For example, the family member with a degree in interior design suddenly finds an interest in designing the interior of automobiles and is invited to early design conversations. The stay-at-home mom realizes she has a passion for getting her PhD in psychotherapy and is offered family resources to do so. The focus of putting the individual first, before the expectations of sacrifice to run the family business or historic assessments of a person's aptitude and interest, allows for more individuality and sustainable unity.

Question 10. Are you taking the necessary steps to become prepared, and are you able to participate fully in family meetings?

You may perceive the family meeting as a waste of your time, and you may find it difficult to be a part of them because of strained relationships. You may find yourself thinking about continuous examples that validate your assessments of why you don't want to be there. It is your responsibility to ask the questions that reveal the larger purpose of family meetings. Having a compelling reason to take time from your own life to support the family mission creates a context for possibilities that will emerge for you, as well as how the generation after you will take on roles. Being prepared to attend these meetings means coming with an open mind, being willing to contribute, and harnessing the emotional strength that may be called on to either disagree or suggest a new direction.

Self-preparation concludes with this challenge: to assume personal responsibility for learning, improving, and using both skills to strengthen not just the family financial assets, but also the asset of the family itself.

Some families value financial assets first, and some value family first. Often financial assets become the default asset. It is an ongoing challenge to maintain family life and family interactions in balance with income-generating responsibilities. Successful families have found their way to achieve and maintain this balance.

Scoring the Individual Family Members' Self-Checklist of Readiness

Using the questions on the self-checklist, you can gauge your personal progress for being prepared for the responsibility of wealth and succession. Fully prepared family members will answer, "yes" to all ten of the checklist questions. This greatly reduces the risk of failure in preparing for and assuming responsibilities for family wealth and values. The worldwide data is incontrovertible—70 percent of wealth transitions will fail.[18]

These generalized preparation questions are also valid for you if you already have a role in financial management or financial management oversight or are actively working in the family enterprise itself, including the family foundation. The above questions can be used as an annual check.

As discussed in chapter 4, simply knowing is insufficient. It is critical to take action to offset the risk of *"shirtsleeves-to-shirtsleeves"* and causing the family estate's demise.

It is an ongoing challenge to maintain family life and family interactions in balance with income-generating responsibilities.

Scores under 7 require active intervention and professional coaching assistance to make the changes necessary to increase the odds of a successful transition.

Your careful preparation, accompanied by *learned* skills and *practiced* behavior of communications and trust within the family, are critical to your success.

Family Team

We often use a football analogy to explain the concept of the family as a high-performing team, with each member understanding his or her contribution to the team and being well-practiced in the "plays" before the wealth actually transfers. The diagram and explanation below illustrate the potential consequences of a scenario that plays out frequently in wealthy families.

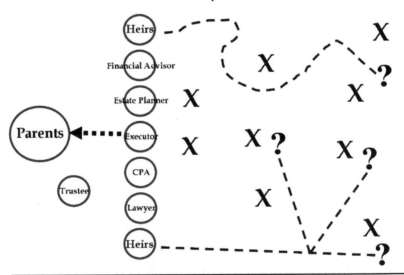

Without Prepared Receivers...

Unprepared Receivers

As a former professional football player, I (Roy) often use a football analogy to illustrate what occurs when family members are unprepared for succession.

To be an effective leader of a football team, the center needs to know the skills of each player and which plays to call for the offensive line. He does so before he snaps the ball on each play.

For the players to know how to play the game, they are first drilled with X's and O's on a blackboard, illustrating potential plays for the field, and then they progress to intrasquad practice on the field prior to the actual game. Through these processes, the team understands the relationships, timing, competencies, capabilities, and shortcomings of each member of the team, thus increasing the possibility of executing successfully.

So it is with preparing family members for success. The executor (center) of the estate (team) needs to know the skills and capabilities of each member and what skills are required for each role so he or she knows what play to call to be an effective leader of the entire line, including lawyers, CPAs, financial advisors, estate planners, and family members.

The family members are the receivers, indicated in the diagram by the dotted lines. If they have never run a football receiver's pattern or caught a ball, (run a business or fulfilled a role), and if they do not know the mission/goal/purpose of the family wealth, how can they play or win? Lying in wait for them are Ponzi schemes, inept advisors, and Bernie Madoffs (defensive players).

Can you imagine your unprepared children and grandchildren playing against the world champions and never having run a play or even having put on a uniform?

To be an effective leader of a football team, the center needs to know the skills of each player and which plays to call for the offensive line.

Receivers and the offensive players practice pass patterns thousands of times. Similarly, heirs need to develop and know the role qualifications and performance standards required to fulfill the family wealth mission and to hire financial advisors.

When do you start to prepare the next generation?

A very distraught man called our office. His grandparents provided him part of their estate in installments at specific ages of 35, 40, 45, 50, and 55. The intent was to allow time and maturity to prepare him to become a better steward of the wealth over time.

He was on several charitable and business boards and was considered a pillar of the community. One of the members of his church convinced him to invest his inheritance in an investment opportunity promising him a 15 percent return so he could give more to charity.

He transferred his $500 million to this investor, based on their mutual church relationship. The investment turned out to be a Ponzi scheme. He lost it all. At the age of seventy-five, he was left with no resources or options to generate income. He had not learned that there needs to be qualification and performance standards for hiring an investment advisor. It does not make any difference whether the amount is $1 or $500 million.

His grandparents' plan was based strictly on chronology, which they thought would protect their grandson by allowing him to mature and learn over time. The conflict we see in families is that many professional advisors think age is a measurement for readiness to receive disbursements, versus developing qualifications and performance standards.

The Williams Advisory Group

Families often request that we educate the next generation on topics including business, investments, estate plans, and philanthropy. The 25 percent factor of preparing the next generations requires specialized attention. Parents, while role models of both good and not-so-good behaviors, often find they cannot coach their own children. It is much easier for objective professionals to help individual heirs identify their needs and interests and introduce them to investing and philanthropy. We created The Williams Advisory Group to answer that call and structured it in a way that allows a portion of asset-management fees to offset part of the cost.

We know that learning happens most effectively when there is a relevant platform of current, live issues for the next generation to address. This allows them to practice being a team while deepening the skills of trust and communication they have learned through The Williams Group Process.

A powerful and relevant way to teach the fundamentals of wealth management is to provide the next generation with investible assets and have them work together to decide the best way to grow that wealth by an agreed-upon percent. They learn how to make decisions as a team about what businesses

Parents, while role models of both good and not-so-good behaviors, often find they cannot coach their own children.

to invest in, how to assess money managers and portfolios, how to read basic financial statements, and develop other skills. A liquidity event may generate a windfall of assets to be managed. The family members may work with the family's current advisor and/or a family mentor to learn these skills, or we may bring in experts to support this process. A Williams Group coach is present throughout the process to ensure that the essential skills of trust and communication, family harmony, and unified action continue to deepen. We keep a steady focus on the importance of the family relationships continuing to grow, not just the wealth itself.

A financial advisor who offers this service to his or her prospects or clients through The Williams Advisory Group requires the family have some assets under management with him or her to offset some of the cost of the service. This fee is usually based on basis points (or part of 1 percent—for example, 50 basis points is 1/2 of 1 percent, and 75 basis points is 3/4 of 1 percent).

Our Preparing Heirs Program builds on, and is an extension of, the values and family wealth mission/purpose phase of our work.

As part of the program, succeeding generation family members play an active role and receive hands-on experience assisting in the implementation of the Family Wealth Mission Statement. Family members work together as a team, learning about philanthropy, wealth management, and the importance of stewardship in sustaining their heritage for future generations.

Building a unified team among the next generation is an essential skill that requires agreed-upon common values, a family mission, trust, and communication skills. Other relevant topics the next generation may be charged with while practicing to function as a team include deciding how to disseminate information about the family business or management of assets to the larger family or creating an on-boarding program for family members who want to enter the family business or manage the family assets or be part of the family philanthropy endeavors. The relevant topics are organically generated by the family and/or the family business, asset management, or philanthropic needs and keep the family members engaged and motivated.

When the family leaders see the power of their family being able to function as a high-performing team, they often want to integrate the power of these practices and tools into their family business's leadership teams.

Family Business Consulting, Coaching, and Advising

When the family leaders see the power of their family being able to function as a high-performing team, they often want to integrate the power of these practices and tools into their family business's leadership teams.

The language of trust, effective partnerships, and shared values can be extended to the executive team of the family business, foundations, boards, asset management, and philanthropy teams. As is true with families, before overlaying the traditional approach of organizational strategy and structure onto a family business, it is important to first address the issues of distrust, cordial hypocrisy (resulting from a hierarchy of power and a lack of clarity of agreed-upon values and mission) that inevitably emerge through the evolution of organizations. Failing to do so results in a shaky foundation that puts future strategy at risk.

Like families, family businesses are each unique and complex. Years of experience provides our team with an understanding of the nuances of working with families and their varied financial interests. Over the past twenty-five years, our partner teams have worked with more than one thousand family-owned businesses.

Harvard Business Review reported in 2012 that 70 percent of family-owned businesses fail or are sold before the second generation has the opportunity to take over, and just 10 percent remain active privately held companies for the third generation to lead.

Many people say family and business don't easily coexist. When these two domains are in competition with each other, one or both suffer. Finding a balance between a passion for the family and a passion for the family business is more easily attained when the two share common values, mission, and trust.

We find that families have more harmony at home and their businesses have a competitive advantage in the marketplace when the values of both are intertwined. Designing a fully integrated plan that aligns the interests of the family with the mission of the business is the bridge that connects the past, present, and future of the family legacy.

Chapter 8 Summary

Included in this chapter is a ten-question checklist for individual family members to use in assessing their self-preparedness for responsibility and accountability for wealth

Over the past twenty-five years, our partner teams have worked with more than one thousand family-owned businesses.

transfer and succession. We discussed the family leader needing to know that asking for family member's input does not mean they are handing over authority or control. It simply means they are willing to listen and make adjustments when it makes sense. One word of caution: it is imperative that the head of the family listen with sincerity to the ideas of the team members. This sets a new pattern of communication and coordination that models more sustainable family engagement and relationships. Ultimately, final decisions still rest with the head of the family.

Self-preparation concludes with this challenge to family members: to assume personal responsibility for learning, improving, and using both skills to strengthen not just the family financial assets but also the asset of the family itself. This requires you also set your own context of relevance for taking on the task of self preparedness.

In this chapter, we provide information about The Williams Advisory Group services for educating the next generation on topics including business, investments, estate plans, and philanthropy.

CHAPTER

9

Why Each Generation Is Really the First

"You never change things by fighting the existing reality. To change something, build a new model that makes the existing model obsolete."

—R. Buckminster Fuller

As the family tree blooms and the number of family members increases exponentially, the family moves further away from the initial generation that created the wealth. When the second, third, fourth, and fifth generations come to be, the resources may be spread across a larger number of people. When the family values are transferred, each generation is as equipped as the first to generate wealth and create opportunities for their own families.

Large, extended families often create a more formal structure to manage relationships among the family, the family business, and the owners. This structure typically includes a family council, a family board, or a family office. Generally, they build a team with other professionals, which often include attorneys, accountants, financial advisors, trust administrators, business consultants, and professionals who specialize in family and personal relationships. These professionals work together to navigate the business, financial and ownership strategy. These areas are interlaced, and to ignore one area causes risk to and affects the other areas.

A vital role of family leaders is to ensure that the next generation has a foundation of family dynamics that is as strong as the strategy and structure of the financial assets. The degree of trust and communication within the family forms the very foundation that supports the infrastructure of governance.

Often, family leaders, being aware of issues within the family that require attention and resolution, do not want the family office staff, whose focus is predominantly strategy and structure, to divert their attention to internal family problems. This is especially true of problems that are outside the expertise of the financial advisors. Advisors often see some of the early signs of discord in family relationships and choose to avoid engaging for fear of stepping outside their area of expertise, or risk losing their job. The signs may be subtle, and sometimes, not so subtle: signs of substance abuse, inability to speak directly to family members (cordial hypocrisy), unresolved issues that underlie communications and interactions for years, entitled behavior, lack of direction and motivation, and moods of resentment and resignation. Parents tend to favor privacy and confidentiality regarding family issues as opposed to having these issues become family office conversations. The rule is privacy and nondisclosure of family issues beyond a need-to-know basis.

A vital role of family leaders is to ensure that the next generation has a foundation of family dynamics that is as strong as the strategy and structure of the financial assets.

Family councils or family boards may desire to engage an outside neutral professional third party to provide support to build stronger family communication strategies and to support the family to work more effectively together. When a family council and board function well as a high-performing team, it role models the expectations and practices that will be carried forward in future generations as younger generations rotate into positions on the board or the council. The skills of having authentic communication while engaging in meaningful conversations, which may be challenging at times, is vital to a high-performing team. Passing along the traditions of how to repair, build, and manage trust in the everyday practices of a family office, council, or board is essential to weaving those qualities into the norm of family relationships.

As we have discussed throughout this book, quite simply put, we see the family as the most vital asset. When the unaddressed rift in families continues to widen, it becomes more challenging to bridge the gap in relationships, and preventative steps are essential to prevent a point of no return. Family rift can dramatically change the activities, environment, leadership, and even impact the ability of a family council, board, or office to operate and even to continue. At the same time, when addressed it can provide an excellent platform for bringing the family together. Within crisis lies opportunity.

Often, by the time a formal structure of communication is required, the family itself has grown quite complex. Without agreed upon family values and a family wealth mission/purpose statement, the family values may get lost as new family members are brought in, the business continues to expand, and the nature of an affluent lifestyle takes hold.

As we have discussed throughout this book, quite simply put, we see the family as the most vital asset.

A family leader who is either skilled, or willing to engage resources with the skills, and who can work in parallel with strengthening the family as a priority and as a vital asset, sets the family up for long term success. Families who are interested in building alignment within the family and succession planning for the next generation are often referred to The Williams Group, primarily through word of mouth, caring friends, and family offices as part of their team. We have excellent references from very prominent families who have experienced our work firsthand, and who volunteered to be open to be contacted in the interest of helping families.

Our skilled and experienced coaches are completely comfortable working through any family issues with family members. They design a learning program for the family to cultivate new communication patterns, support the family members to arrive at their own solutions, and then take action based on a shared commitment to the family values and mission. Through these processes, families develop and deepen family bonding to become a unified team. A new pattern of communication practices is woven into future generations. As Buckminster Fuller, a renowned twentieth-century inventor and visionary would say, a new model is built.

The Customized Family Office

Families today are looking for more customized services, and many are asking for resources to support the family as a whole. Multifamily offices are now offering up to thirty different products and services.

However, a 2014 study[18] of eighty-nine multifamily offices reported in an article titled "What Is a Family Office?" that families actually used few of these services. Their research indicated that 70 percent of the services used were singularly investment management-related. The next most popular services used by 53 percent of families involved estate, financial, charitable, and succes-

---

18. "What Is a 'Multifamily Office'?" R. A. Prince, H. S. Grove, and R. J. Flynn, *Financial Advisor* magazine 236 (November 7, 2014), http://www.fa-mag.com/news/what-is-a--multifamily-office-19781.html?issue=236.

sion planning. Today the trend is for multifamily offices to offer core products and services and to craft customized solutions through strategic outsourcing that meets the needs of each individual family. Other trends mentioned in the 2015 Global Family Office report[19] highlights a higher tendency toward riskier asset categories and higher costs (92 to 99 basis points of AUM).

Advisors who can bring customized solutions to their clients, including services that address the family's relationship dynamics, will better serve the family long term and extend the longevity of the family office. Advisors have an opportunity to position themselves as offering both sides of the asset equation: the financial and the family.

Below are recommended actions a family can take to ensure a formal structure of communication that will support their family in the most vital way. These actions will foster trust and communication within the generations to ensure a sustainable legacy:

Advisors have an opportunity to position themselves as offering both sides of the asset equation: the financial and the family.

1. **The entire eligible family, instead of just Mom and Dad, decides on the needs, roles, and performance standards required to run your family office.** Are you seeking a team that will simply focus on strategy and structure, or do you also want family members who will be comfortable addressing the vital issues of family harmony and team building? Or are you looking for both? Also, there may be roles within the family office, board, or council that would provide an opportunity for family members to explore their

19. Campden Wealth and UBS, "Family Offices 2015–More Risk, Lower Performance, Higher Costs." Global Family Office Report 2015, Themes, http://Globalfamilyofficereport.com, http://www.campdenfb.com/article/over-third-family-office-ceos-are-female-says-research, http://www.globalfamilyofficereport.com/.

own aspirations and develop competence. Or
there may be a role for someone to learn to assess
the competence and value of advisors, oversee the
return on investments, and be the liaison to the
rest of the family.

2. **The entire family is included in the discussions and process, including age-eligible offspring and their spouses/partners.** It is
equally important to agree, as a family, on the
values to be used to set policy and direction for
the family. If the family office, board, or council
is to exist beyond the current family leader's
reign, then it is important for the entire family to
be aligned with the values that form the foundation for the family office, board, or council. The
leader you select for the family management is a
manifestation of the family values. A sole focus
on strategy and structure reflects emphasis on
asset management, while a consigliore approach
widens the focus to include family relationships,
family values, and family mission.

3. **Agreement on the family wealth mission/ purpose will galvanize the family in a specific direction.** Building alignment with how the
family governance will perpetuate the values in
everyday actions and decisions is vital to the family's success. Declaring a purpose for the wealth
ensures that the wealth does not declare the purpose. For example, younger generations are easily
overwhelmed by the choices available to them as
a result of the wealth. A shared purpose enables
coherent philanthropy and investment strategies
and clear expectations regarding everything from

education to distributions, and it often enables adrift heirs to find meaningful work supported by the family.

4. **Establishing an open environment for trust and communication is vital.** When the need for a formal family communication structure is identified, it is because the wealth of the family has reached new heights of financial prosperity and complexity and the family has grown so large that communicating to the entire family has become

The leader you select for the family office management is a manifestation of the family values.

unwieldy. The family is dealing with new horizons of possibilities with respect to charity and/ or philanthropy, exponentially growing family members, blending families with more demands, forming a more expansive advisor network to coordinate, and developing a bigger identity to manage in the community, among other things. This new landscape requires new skills to navigate. The skills of communication and relationship that have allowed the family to reach this point in their trajectory are unlikely to be the same skills that will carry them through a wealth transition and succession into the next generation. Learning new ways of engaging, in addition to the ones they already have, allows families to grow even stronger. It is inevitable that there are conversations that have been suppressed for fear of hurting someone's feelings, or lack of knowledge about how to carry out a policy fairly, how to invite two-way communication to allow voices to be heard, or having confidence that the family office, council, or board is serving the family in ways that support the very family it is designed to serve.

5. **Select an external family office executive.** According to Jane Flanagan, Director of Family Research and the Family Office Exchange study,[20] finding and retaining talent is the number one concern for family offices. Having family members participate in the search and the interview process will build consensus and buy-in.

6. **The family should use well-developed qualification and performance standards, as well as interview questions, as a screening and monitoring tool to assist in assessing a candidate's competence and fit with the family culture.** This process will reveal the family members' comfort level and competence in dealing with the core issues responsible for enabling a family to thrive.

Learning new ways of engaging, in addition to the ones they already have, allows families to grow even stronger.

Finding the Right Leader for the Family Office

Hiring the right person skilled at both expert financial and asset management and family dynamics can seem like a daunting challenge. The process itself provides an opportunity to begin to engage family members in new ways. First, the family can decide as a team what the goals of the family office are, define how the family values and mission will be lived through the interface with the family of-

---

20. "Family Office Compensation Expected to Increase by 3 Percent in 2016," Family Office Exchange website, press release, October 28, 2015, https://www.familyoffice.com/press-releases/family-office-compensation-expected-increase-3-percent-2016.

fice, and have the family members themselves develop the services they would find most valuable.

Defining the leadership of the family office affects the recruitment process enormously, says Kathryn McCarthy, a leading New York-based family office consultant and director of the Rockefeller Trust company.[21]

Asking the right questions of prospective and even current family office leaders reveals their level of competence, commitment, and alignment with the role of a "consigliore" versus one that comes from a traditional frame of strategy and structure. Hiring the right head of a family office can provide much more than excellent management and investment services. It is an opportunity to be a blessing to the growth and development of the family and the future generations.

Below are a few suggested interview questions designed to reveal the values, competence, and commitment of a potential candidate:

1. What in your background qualifies you for this assignment?

2. What type of education do you provide the younger family generations? How do you deliver it?

3. What examples can you offer about how you have handled disagreements among family board members?

4. What is your philosophy regarding transparency, accountability, and participation?

5. How do you manage the power gradient between the family leader and the next generation and ensure that their voices are heard?

---

21. "The Next Generation of Family Office Leadership," SpencerStuart website, https://www.spencerstuart.com/research-and-insight/the-next-generation-of-family-office-leadership.

6. What metrics do you put in place to assess your own performance?

7. How do you know you are satisfying the needs of the entire family, not just the family leader?

8. When do you know when and what kinds of issues to bring to the board and/or family leader?

9. How have you dealt with issues you see developing in the family regarding their individual relationships with each other?

10. To what extent have you developed agreed-upon roles, standards for qualification and performance, and rules of engagement between the family office leader and the family leader? These will delineate how decisions will be made to prevent any violations of family governance.

11. What resources have you used effectively in the past to meet the challenge of this type of work? Cite examples.

Hiring the right head of a family office can provide much more than excellent management and investment services. It is an opportunity to be a blessing to the growth and development of the family and the future generations.

These questions are designed to broaden the scope of a candidate's capacity and competence beyond the traditional frame of strategy and structure. Although these questions are often ignored through the interview process because of the challenges often associated with family dynamics, it is imperative that you address them. When family office executives respond to these questions in a way that aligns with the family needs and culture, they will be in the best possible position to serve the family well for the long term.

Hiring the right head of a family office can provide much more than excellent management and investment services. This person is also aware of resources that can serve the family needs. Having the right person at the helm is a blessing to the growth and development of the family and future generations.

Chapter 9 Summary

In an evolving large, extended family, just like a corporate office, the leadership and the family need to have the same values, goals, and high level of trust to be successful. This will allow the family bond to strengthen and operate within a transparent environment, resulting in a successful family governance structure.

The focus of family management, which is narrowly constricted to simply communicating or managing wealth, is missing a central component that can help ensure family prosperity. Dating as far back as there have been family offices, the forces of a lack of prepared family members, undefined family values and mission, and inability to develop trust are the harbingers of lost assets and divided families.

Families who are committed to "best in class" succession planning can learn proactively to build new, healthy practices of communication that allow the family to thrive well into the future. These skills provide protection for the family's long-term relationships and assets. In the family office structure, hiring the right leader with this understanding, and who is willing to partner with a family at this level, is indispensable.

CHAPTER

10

Your Legacy

"I have found the best way to give advice to your children is to find out what they want and advise them to do it."

—Harry S. Truman

Every time we experience a family successfully cultivating the skill sets required to ensure a successful wealth transfer and succession, we find ourselves wishing this for all families. Many times, we have witnessed the comfort and closeness this type of proactive preparation brings to family members. Ultimately, families desire family unity and harmony. We trust the stories we share from other families offer insight and inspire you to begin the rewarding and exciting process of strengthening your family unity. We encourage you to join the growing ranks of families who are beating the odds typical of wealth transfer and achieving successful wealth and succession transitions.

In the pages of these chapters, we have highlighted the challenges that can come with wealth transfers, and we have provided tried and proven steps you can take to cultivate the skills necessary to unify your family and ensure that your legacy will continue for future generations. You can answer the vital question of whether your wealth will divide or unify your family by focusing on family values and mission and developing the skills to build trust and communication.

When each generation accepts the responsibility of carrying forth their family values, raising responsible stewards of wealth, and making a conscious effort to manage relationships, *the family leads the wealth, as opposed to the wealth leading the family.* When families are aligned, we have seen them make grand contributions in the world as an extension of their values and commitment to their legacy having a significant impact.

We have distilled our fifty-two-plus years of investigating how successful families transition their wealth into five steps the family can take. This five-step process has withstood the test of time and continues to add value and applies to families today:

The family leads the wealth, as opposed to the wealth leading the family.

- First Step: Leadership—Taking the Initiative to Beat the Odds (Here's Your Road Map)

- Second Step: Securing Your Wealth Transition Plan

- Third Step: Turning Wealth-Transition-Plan Deficiencies into an Action Plan for Success

- Fourth Step: Preparing Your Family Members

- Fifth Step: Family Members' Self-Preparation Responsibilities

Perhaps the most profound discovery we have learned over the years is that the most powerful source of wealth is not found in the balance sheet. *The power of wealth exists in the family itself,* its history and the norms and practices of that family to build trust with one another, encourages the passions of each individual to be pursued and supported, and a commitment from all to form a high-performing team for the sake of long-term wealth and family unity preservation. The prerequisite is, of course, love and care, both of which are nurtured when the family is the primary focus.

Elusive words like love, care, and trust can be difficult to define. We speak about them as if they exist as things. You treasure the love you have for someone, you either have trust or you don't, and we provide care for others. These attributes are defined by the actions taken or not taken that characterize family relationships, as opposed to a thing that actually exists. To say you trust your brother is witnessed, measured, and perpetuated in the willingness to have open and honest conversations, a commitment to put family first before business, the acts of forgiveness and acceptance, etc. To invite a conversation with the child who is considered the successor to the family business and explore if that is really what the child wants is an act of love and care. To be willing to engage in meaningful conversations about your expectations of your children is a skill that provides an opportunity for conflict to be generative and opens new possibilities not considered before.

When families are aligned, we have seen them make grand contributions in the world as an extension of their values and commitment to their legacy having a significant impact.

We propose that the skills of observing, repairing, and managing love, care and trust can be learned. Learning is most effective when it is relevant. Integrating a family culture that promotes learning as the norm eliminates the pressure that comes when we expect the next generation to already know how to manage their wealth or read financial statements. Such a family

Learning is most effective when it is relevant.

culture encourages them to ask when they don't know what is expected of them.

Educating the next generation reduces the likelihood that they will be captive to their trusts, prepares them to embrace taking on the helm of leading the family and family business, and enables them to continue sowing the seeds of prosperity. This is where the leverage lies for generational wealth. Although excellent governance will ensure a degree of preservation and governance, a focus on both strategy and structure *and* the family is required.

Philanthropy is one of the best teachers for enabling younger members of the next generation to learn the family values and put them into action. It can be how a family rebuilds family pride and strengthens its legacy. It also can be a conduit for a family member who is distanced from the rest of the family as he or she finds a common purpose and rebuilds relationships.

Philanthropy is one of the best teachers for enabling younger members of the next generation to learn the family values and put them into action.

Families are meant to be enjoyed and celebrated. *Family is our true wealth*—ask any grandparent! Recognizing the family itself as the true wealth provides the entire family with a bigger picture and meaning far beyond money and assets, which then become secondary in importance. *Money and material things do not determine who you are—your values and relationships do.*

All solutions begin with a desired outcome in mind and progress to a move to action. No one likes to admit they are headed for a crash, especially when they are at the end of a first-generation wealth-building process. Pride of achievement may have set in. Knowing you have done

Knowing you have done the best you can to provide for your family is a landmark moment.

the best you can to provide for your family is a landmark moment.

And that is where the next level of responsibility begins that accompanies wealth.

You've taken a major step toward success by reading this book. Despite the hundreds of well-coached family transitions we have examined, the feedback we hear is that the value gained associated with this kind of process is worth far more than the financial investment. It is difficult to put a price on the peace that comes with intergenerational family harmony and prosperity.

Based on your family needs, seek outside assistance from professionals who specialize in preparing families and developing family unity in the process. The process of selecting a coach is detailed in chapter 6.

We encourage you to make the commitment today to take the steps that will lead to the very best outcome for you and your family.

Sincerely,
Roy Williams and Amy Castoro

APPENDIX

1

The Williams Group Research and Field Studies

For a number of years, The Williams Group had substantial success in the estate and financial planning arena, primarily based on our *values-based estate* and financial planning process.

Financially successful clients repeatedly asked us to help them with their heirs: "How do we prepare our children?" As The Williams Group client base grew nationwide, we saw that in spite of the fact that the best legal, tax, and financial advisors developed excellent estate and financial *plans*, the family fell apart when the parents died.

In trying to find out what was behind this consistent pattern of failure, we began our research. We sought out legal and tax advisors, psychologists, and business consultants. We found that everyone, including The Williams Group, was focused on strategy and structure of preservation, governance, and tax-reduction techniques.

The Executive Committee International (TEC) is an organization formed to help business owners learn from one another. Among the basic tenets of the organization are confidentiality, openness of communication, sharing, and willingness to learn from peers or guest speakers. TEC Chapters consist of ten to fifteen CEOs or business owners, none of which would be directly competitive. These chapters meet monthly to exchange information and develop deeper relationships. TEC chapters are sprinkled across the United States and worldwide. TEC has thousands of chapters, mostly representing medium- to large-sized (closely held) companies. We began our research by asking TEC groups what was successful or unsuccessful in the transition of their own companies (or wealth). Some were second- and third-generation owners, and others were founders/first-generation owners.

Over the next twenty years, The Williams Group interviewed a thousand business owners and clients (some of whom managed only asset pools) to ascertain what worked and what did not. Additionally, over time we interviewed another 1,500 individuals who had experienced failures in their family succession and were referred by the business owners.

As a member of TEC, I (Roy) was allowed to ask questions of members who would normally be unavailable to answer, or reluctant to answer a nonpeer. Because of the organizational and direct relationship, as well as the well-known confidentiality component of membership, we found members very open in their responses.

In addition, The Williams Group's background in estate and financial planning equipped me to ask focused questions, and, depending on the response, to delve deeper into the answers to identify the core or causal issues. A pattern emerged as a distinct set of consistent principles underlying both successful and failed estate transitions. Here are those underlying factors:

The first factor is a breakdown of communication within the family, and its root cause is a lack of trust within the family. This is a consistent feature of almost all failed transitions. An example of this communication breakdown is heirs being uninformed of the parental estate plan or transition plan, how much money the parents earned, or even the family's net worth.

Our research revealed that family advisors typically have full access to such information, and the next generation knows of that access, which leaves them with the feeling of being perceived as less trustworthy than the advisors. Many of the parent(s) said, "I don't want to create a disincentive for them by letting them know how much they will inherit" or "If I tell them, they will be waiting for me to die so they can have access to the money." The excuses indicated a lack of trust within the family. Where trust did not exist, families consistently demonstrated very little open communication.

When The Williams Group began interviewing the second and third generations, we found that these generations clearly recognized the same problems. They stated, "Why didn't my dad trust me enough to tell me what he had planned before he died, so I could be prepared?" or "My brother or sister have no interest or involvement in the business, yet they own two-thirds of the company, receive two-thirds of the distributions, and resent my salary and company car, which are part of my employment with the family company!"

Repeatedly, there is no clear understanding among the siblings (of failed transitions) concerning the concepts of "sweat equity" or the fact that a salary and perks have to be paid to a nonfamily member employed in the business. While the stories were varied, the theme was the same: no trust, and therefore, little communication.

The second factor that emerged during these interviews was the lack of preparation of the family.

The research indicates that, often, planning for the next generations only goes as far as their college attendance. Many family members learn of their role when the lawyer reads the will, *after* the head of the family has died. Almost all are totally unprepared. Many spent years learning on the job without a mentor. They lack understanding of the qualifications advisors need. Some rely on family professional advisors, only to learn that a good trial lawyer or good CPA auditor does not necessarily make a good investment advisor. An advisor may or may not possess any particular business skill in running a company.

In many cases, family and friends earnestly try to help, but they lack competence in managing wealth, resulting in various unintended consequences. This creates more mistrust, miscommunication, disputes, and lawsuits.

In successful estate transitions, trust based on competence is reinforced by more trust and confidence in family members' judgment.

We also found that the need for control, stemming from a fear of loss of money, power, influence, etc., is offset over time by increasing trust. This manifestation of trust by family leaders, in the judgment and competence of family members, proves to be a stimulus to further efforts to develop even better judgment and even more competence. It is a positive and affirming cycle that builds on itself. This leads to more open communication and disclosure of information. Accountability, reliability, and commitment are the ways family members are measured. Knowing this, standards are set and agreed on.

The third factor we found to be consistent (among failed transitions) was the lack of clarity in "roles" that might be available to family members in the management of family assets. This was especially harmful when family members wish to make a contribution to the family and demonstrate interest, yet no effort is made to match a role with their talents and interests. A well-developed family wealth mission and strategy/structure leads to the identification of possible roles for family members. With the absence of a family wealth mission, needed roles are not identified, nor are observable or measurable standards established for fulfilling roles. We found no business or family that remained unified (in subsequent generations) if they lacked agreed-upon family values, a family wealth mission, and authentic trust. The steady rise in divorce rates and family dissolution are broader examples of this phenomenon.

Research Group Sizes and Participants

The family size researched ranged from one child to twenty-two children and spouses. The average composition of all 2,500 families was three children, with 1.5 being married. Their ages ranged from eight to sixty-eight.

For the study, we interviewed 2,500 individuals. Eighty percent were leaders of closely held operating businesses, and 20 percent were owners and managers of cash, securities, and real property interests. The families we studied had net worth ranging from just under $5 million to well over $1 billion, with the average range between $15 million and $70 million.

Of the families, 70 percent were first-generation, and 30 percent were second- or third-generation managers of wealth and/or business. The first-generation managers had a 20 percent divorce rate. The second- and third-generation managers had a 40 percent divorce rate. The largest family surveyed had twelve members, and the smallest had three members (plus spouses and/or grandchildren). The geographic locations of the businesses surveyed were fairly evenly distributed across the United States. The primary locations were California, Texas, New York, Florida, and Canada.

APPENDIX

2

Sample Family Wealth Mission Statements

To use our resources to strengthen our family and to support causes in which we believe.

We are committed to family bonding, community outreach, and fun. We grow the family assets and provide for the family's education, growth, and security.

To create an environment for making choices that benefit us and the world for generations to come.

To maximize the equitable transfer of my assets in a way that will enable and encourage my heirs to work for the benefit of humanity.

Through God's grace, dream, plan, and grow closer to God and each other using the resources entrusted to our care for the benefit of God's work, family, business people, and community.

To strengthen our family and use its assets wisely; to enable our family and others to realize their fullest potential; to value and encourage love, work, self-sufficiency, and cooperation within the family and in the larger community.

3

Additional Resources

Coaching

The Williams Group provides family coaching to support family members in increasing their communication skill level; strengthening family unity and harmony; identifying their agreed-upon family values, and based on these values, developing the family wealth mission/purpose statement; comparing the family wealth mission/purpose and estate plans for alignment; and identifying needs the family has and roles to meet those needs, along with qualification and performance standards for roles. Family meetings are conducted at the family's location of choice. To discover whether The Williams Group may be of help, please contact us at U.S. +1 (949) 940-9140 or at www.thewilliamsgroup.org.

50-Question Family Readiness Survey, © 2001 by The Williams Group

This anonymous fifty-question Family Readiness Assessment is to be completed by *all family members and spouses* and submitted to The Williams Group for analysis and scoring. The results will be provided in a detailed, written report that shows differences among family members that may contribute to an unsuccessful post-transition. Anonymity of respondents is protected at all times, and each participating family member will receive a copy of the seven-page customized report. Contact The Williams Group for pricing.

Philanthropy Heirs & Values by Roy Williams and Vic Pressier, © 2005 by The Williams Group

The full title of this book is *How Successful Families Are Using Philanthropy to Prepare Their Heirs for Post-Transition Responsibilities.* After interviewing 3,250 families and examining almost 100 foundations, this book discloses how successful families use philanthropy as a teaching tool to improve their odds of post-transition success. Their children learn *values,* develop appreciation for a specific *mission,* and are instilled with a sense of *accountability.* The authors provide exercises, examples, and checklists for each of five age groups.

THE WILLIAMS GROUP

We prepare heirs

Preparing Families For Successful Wealth Transition Since 1964.

The Williams Group has been equipping families, businesses, and foundations with the trust and communication skills needed for proactive, successful wealth transition.

Contact us today to get a snapshot of how prepared your family is by taking the Family Readiness Assessment Survey.

PROGRAMS INCLUDE:

- Family Readiness Assessment
- The Williams Group Process
- One on one family member coaching
- Private briefing speaking engagements

If you choose to put into practice what you have just read, contact us for more information.

Visit www.thewilliamsgroup.org to learn more about our work, family coaches, find other informative publications, and read our blogs. Also, be sure to sign up for our quarterly newsletter.

Share...

If you have enjoyed this book, share your thoughts on Amazon, Goodreads, and post a positive review! The Williams Group will gift you another book as our way of thanking you for your time.

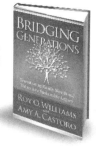

NOTES

NOTES

NOTES

NOTES

NOTES